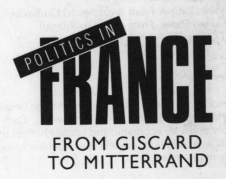

POLITICS IN FRANCE

FROM GISCARD TO MITTERRAND

About the Series

Chambers Political Spotlights aim to provide a bridge between
conventional textbooks and contemporary reporting. Each title
examines the key political, economic and social changes of the
country, providing, in addition, a brief contextual background to
each development discussed.

CHAMBERS POLITICAL SPOTLIGHTS

POLITICS IN FRANCE

FROM GISCARD TO MITTERRAND

Ian Derbyshire
Ph.D. Cantab

Chambers

© Ian Derbyshire 1987

First published by Sandpiper Publishing as a Sandpiper Compact, 1986
This edition published by W & R Chambers Ltd, 1987
Reprinted 1988

British Library Cataloguing in Publication Data

Derbyshire, Ian
  Politics in France: from Giscard to
  Mitterrand.—(Chambers political
  spotlights).
  1. France—Politics and government—
  1969-
  I. Title
  320.944   JN2594.2

  ISBN 0-550-20744-9

Typeset by Bookworm Typesetting Limited, 9a Gayfield Square, Edinburgh
Printed in Great Britain at the University Press, Cambridge

Acknowledgements

This book is based on a wide range of contemporary sources including
*The Times, The Guardian, The Independent, The Observer, The Sunday
Times, The Economist, Newsweek, Time, Keesing's Contemporary
Archives, The Annual Register* and *Europa: A World Survey*.

Figures 2 and 3 by permission of *The Economist*

Every effort has been made to trace copyright holders, but if any have
inadvertently been overlooked the publishers will be pleased to make the
necessary arrangements at the first opportunity.

Contents

Contents

Preface

In May 1974 the young, 48-year-old, technocrat, Valéry Giscard d'Estaing, was elected the Fifth Republic's third President following a knife-edged electoral contest. Giscard entered office promising a new era of liberal reform to update the Gaullist rule. He was to leave office in May 1981 an embittered figure, having experienced seven years of intra-coalition strife and buffeting by a severe economic recession. His successor, François Mitterrand, became the Fifth Republic's first Socialist President. He secured an Assembly majority for his party in June 1981 and sought in the succeeding two years to radically and decisively transform the French polity and economy. Mitterrand's reform efforts were, however, like Giscard's, to be overwhelmed by events. In March 1983 he was forced to introduce an austerity U-turn programme and three years later his party lost its Assembly majority, thrusting France into a novel and experimental period of 'cohabitation'.

This Spotlight examines the key changes in the French polity during the last decade. It looks at the varying fortunes of France's major parties and ideological coalitions; changing policy prescriptions; and the dominant personalities and issues. In particular, it examines the modernisation and liberalisation of the inherited Gaullist state and focuses in depth on both the 1981-85 'Socialist Experiment' and the post-1986 'cohabitation' experience.

FIGURE 1   THE REGIONS OF FRANCE

Part One

THE FRENCH POLITICAL SYSTEM

France — A Divided Society?

France, bordered to the south by the Pyrenees, to the east by the Alps, Jura, Vosges and Ardennes, and to the north and west by the Atlantic Ocean, has long formed a settled and distinct nation state. Provinces on its eastern and southern borders have periodically been ceded during wars with neighbouring nations, but for more than five centuries the major portion of contemporary France has been ruled as a single entity. It has enjoyed a shared culture and language and has predominantly followed Roman Catholicism. Despite these geographical and cultural bonds, however, France has not been a politically united nation. Social and regional antagonisms have remained powerful and have frequently exploded into violent and revolutionary conflicts, resulting in sudden changes in regime.

Regional divisions have always remained significant in a country which, covering 213 000 square miles, is more than twice the size of the United Kingdom or West Germany and whose climate and topography exhibit a tremendous diversity. Economic and social divisions have also been wide. During the *ancien régime*, an absolutist monarchy and provincial aristocracy dominated French society and the middle orders of the gentry and commercial *bourgeoisie* remained attenuated. Industrial and urban development came late in the 19th century and was uneven. This left French society unusually dominated by rural and small town interests up to the 1950s and fostered income differentials amongst the broadest in Europe. Finally, ideological differences have been stark and firmly held in a nation which, in contrast to the pragmatic and consensual utilitarianism of the United Kingdom, has been suffused with utopian philosophical idealism.

1

During the 17th and greater part of the 18th century, the powerful and centralised Bourbon monarchy, served by a dependent aristocracy and by a relatively efficient administrative system, held French society together. However, criticism of the autocratic nature of this regime mounted from the 1750s, leading to its overthrow by a combination of the nobility, the bourgeoisie and the Paris mob during the Revolution which began in 1789. The country experimented with a variety of liberal, democratic and totalitarian government forms during the ensuing decade and has been searching for the ideal institution ever since: 17 different constitutions having been framed in the years since 1789.

Throughout the post-revolution period the country has been bitterly divided between those on the Left who have favoured the transfer of power to a democratic, representative and republican legislature (*gouvernement d'assemblée*) and who have sought to foster effective local government, individual and press freedom and secularism, and those on the Right who have sought order, stability and unity through a strong, autocratic and centralised executive form of administration, buttressed by a respected Catholic church. These differing goals have frequently proved to be unbridgeable and resulted in violent revolutions and attempted coups in 1830, 1848, 1851, 1870, 1877, 1889 and 1934 and chronic political instability during the terms of the Third and Fourth Republics between 1870 and 1958.

The Flawed Third and Fourth Republics

France experimented with a system of plebiscitary autocracy under the two Napoleons between 1799-1814 and 1851-1870 and with a constitutional monarchy between 1815-1848. In 1870 the nation embarked on a new experiment: that of parliamentary democracy. A bicameral political system was established in this, the Third Republic (1870-1940), moulded on the British and American models. The lower house, the Chamber of Deputies, was elected for fixed four-year terms through a system of universal manhood suffrage and was granted the most extensive legislative powers. The upper chamber, the Senate, was elected indirectly by *département* and municipal councillors, and was never dissolved, each deputy serving a nine-year term with a third retiring in rotation every three years. It had substantial delaying and veto powers on the model of the British House of Lords. Both chambers jointly elected a

President as nominal head of the executive to serve a seven-year term, but he required ministerial approval for any legislative acts attempted.

The Third Republic's (unwritten) constitution was advanced by the standards of the late 19th century with its rejection of the idea of a monarchy and its extension of the franchise to all male adults. It proved, however, in many respects to be too liberal, granting too great a power to individual legislature members and creating too weak a policy-framing executive. Deputies inside the parliamentary chambers were given extensive powers to debate issues, put forward bills and amendments, shape legislation through their work on the lower chamber's 19 specialised legislative commissions, and block unpalatable bills in the upper house. Matters were compounded by the weakness and multiplicity of political parties during the Third Republic, which resulted from the nation's social and ideological divisions, economic backwardness and the slow spread of communications. Politics were thus unusually individualistic during this period, with deputies and senators being concerned above all to uphold local constituency interests.[1] Conservative-liberal and centre party groups orientated towards rural and small town electorates dominated the two chambers, but it proved difficult to construct regular majority coalitions. Governments were, therefore, frequently overturned, with over 100 administrations holding office between 1870 and 1940. There was greater continuity in terms of cabinet membership, while the civil service provided a vital source of stability. In general, however, the Third Republic was a period of policy *immobilisme*, with strong similarities to the US Congressional system during periods of weak presidential leadership and to the 'stalled' Italian political system.

When the French political system was reconstructed after the German occupation during the Second World War, a deliberate effort was made to overcome the weaknesses of the previous regime. The interventionary powers of the President and upper chamber (now termed the Council of the Republic) were much reduced and the authority of the Prime Minister and his cabinet in the lower chamber (National Assembly) was augmented in an effort to construct a strong executive form of government while maintaining the legislature checks to be found in the British system. In addition, a new electoral system, comprising large, multi-

[1] Deputies were elected into single-member constituencies by the two-ballot majority-plurality system employed later during the Fifth Republic.

member *département* constituencies and a 'party list', proportional representation voting procedure, was introduced in an effort to encourage the emergence of larger, national party groupings and to reduce deputies' dependence upon constituency interest groups.

However, despite these efforts to create a stronger executive form of government, French social conditions were still unable to support a classic two-party form of government. A multiplicity of party groupings, divided over the varied issues of economic and social policy, church schools, the French Empire and European unification, vied for supremacy in the National Assembly, while a third of the delegates (the Communists and extreme Gaullist and Poujadist right) rejected the constitutional, parliamentary approach to politics. This meant that government instability was marked once more during the Fourth Republic. There were 26 separate cabinets and 15 different Prime Ministers between 1946 and 1958. Interest groups were thus able to dominate the National Assembly's legislative commissions while faceless bureaucrats were left to administer the nation in the politicians' absence.

The Political System of the Fifth Republic

The Fourth Republic was overthrown in May-June 1958 by a political and military crisis over Algeria. A bitter war of independence had been raging there since November 1954 and it appeared that the resolve of the Paris government was beginning to waver by 1958. The French army in Algeria, whose officer corps was dominated by traditional ultra-rightists, were determined, however, to preserve the *tricoleur* in Algeria. They fomented a settlers' insurrection and threatened to invade mainland France and bring down the centrist government. The Fourth Republic's politicians thus turned in desperation to the forceful and charismatic figure of General Charles de Gaulle, the former Free French leader and head of the 1945/6 provisional government, as the only person able to control the army, solve the Algerian issue and maintain national unity.

De Gaulle's assumption of power represented a coup by those parties of the Right who had been excluded from office for much of the period of the Third and Fourth Republics. It also presaged, however, a major transformation of the French political system, with a new constitution being constructed which attempted to combine elements of the country's two political traditions of strong executive leadership and democratic, legislative accountability.

This new constitution was hastily framed within three months of de Gaulle's assumption of power and was approved by 79% of the French population in a referendum held on 28 September 1958. It was an ambiguous constitution, drawn up by the Justice Minister Michel Debré, which sought to combine elements of the American and British political systems and, above all, to strengthen the executive's authority and encourage the emergence of a smaller number of disciplined political parties. The constitution visualised the creation of a twin-headed executive consisting of a President, to be elected indirectly every seven years by a college of 80 000 municipal and département councillors, and a Prime Minister and cabinet (Council of Ministers). The powers of the President were significantly augmented in the new constitution. He held the titles of head of state and commander-in-chief of the armed forces, appointed the Prime Minister, enjoyed the right to dissolve the National Assembly once a year, presided over cabinet and Defence Council meetings, countersigned government bills, received ambassadors, negotiated treaties, and controlled military, judicial and administrative appointments. However, it was the Prime Minister and Council of Ministers, responsible to the National Assembly, who were to exert ultimate control over policy-making in the Fifth Republic according to Articles 20 and 21 of the constitution. The President was meant rather to play an aloof and backstage role as a 'fixer' who cemented together the participants in the ruling coalition and as the guardian and final arbiter of the constitution, in accordance with Article 5.

In practice, however, the President emerged as the dominant political and policy-making figure in the Fifth Republic as a result of the activities of the first President, Charles de Gaulle, and the acquiescence of the Prime Minister and National Assembly. De Gaulle sought a powerful executive role for himself with the Prime Minister and Council of Ministers acting merely as his parliamentary agents. He thus, unconstitutionally, forced through, by referendum, a change in the constitution in October 1962 to enable the President to be elected directly by universal suffrage. This transformed the political scene and the power balance between President and Prime Minister. De Gaulle, supported by his own majority party, proceeded to dominate French politics from the Élysée Palace during the next seven years and created a new paramount role for the presidency. His successors have built and, in places, extended this role, making the President the crucial and controlling figure in French politics, at least until March 1986.

Organs of Executive Power

The President emerged as the dominant figure in the complicated French executive structure during the years between 1958 and 1976 in what has been termed a 'hyper-presidential system'. Any person able to muster 500 signatures from elected officials in at least 30 départements is eligible to contest the seven-yearly presidential election, but in practice the office has been monopolised by leaders of either the Right or Left majority party coalitions. More than ten party leaders usually contest the first ballot of the presidential contest, but with no single candidate being able, thus far, to secure more than 50% of the vote, the election has been decided by a second ballot head-to-head battle between two contenders from the Right and Left. (See Table 1)

TABLE 1 : PRESIDENTIAL ELECTIONS (2nd Ballot), 1965-81							
	1965		1969		1974		1981	
	De Gaulle	Mitterrand	Pompidou	Poher	Giscard	Mitterrand	Giscard	Mitterrand
	(Right)	(Left)	(Right)	(Centre)	(Right)	(Left)	(Right)	(Left)
% OF VOTE	54.5	45.5	57.6	42.4	50.7	49.3	48.2	51.8
(Turnout)	(85%)		(69%)		(88%)		(86%)	

Once installed in office, the President chooses a Prime Minister from the majority coalition and supervises the subsequent choice of the ministerial team. If a President assumes office at a time when his party or coalition is in the minority he will dissolve the National Assembly and call on the voters to furnish a suitable legislature in the ensuing parliamentary elections: this François Mitterrand successfully achieved in 1981. Only since March 1986 has a President faced, after midterm parliamentary elections, a National Assembly dominated by the opposition coalition and been forced to choose a Prime Minister against his natural inclinations.

In the period prior to March 1986 a President working with a compliant Prime Minister and National Assembly was able to control decisively the executive apparatus. Supported by a private office (General Staff) of political troubleshooters and technocrat administrative advisers, the President gave broad instructions to his

Prime Minister and ministerial colleagues and presided over ministerial and specialised committees (for example, the Central Planning Council, the Environment Committee and the Defence Committee). He ruled in a manner akin to that of the American President, without being subject to the extensive legislative, judicial and provincial checks evident in the American system. De Gaulle, being little interested in economic affairs, concentrated his personal attention on the area constitutionally specified to be of particular presidential concern, foreign affairs. However, his successors, Pompidou, Giscard d'Estaing and Mitterrand, extended the President's personal interest into economic and social spheres, thus creating an all-pervasive system of Élysée control.

Apart from working through his prime ministerial and cabinet team, the President has been supported by an unusually skilled and influential corps of official administrative personnel. France pioneered the creation of an effective bureaucratic system during the seventeenth century and has boasted a powerful administrative élite ever since. The top cadres of this élite are rigorously trained at the *École Nationale d'Administration (ENA)* and *École Polytechnique* and have played a major role in policy making: the Fifth Republic has been termed a 'technocrats' paradise'. They are unusually politicised by British standards, many serving in local government and ministerial cabinets or leaving to become Assembly deputies. Their careers are thus dramatically altered by each Right-Left change in political power.

Presidents have also periodically acted in a more direct and personal manner, bypassing traditional parliamentary and administrative channels. They have used the television medium to make national enquiries and reports, while de Gaulle, who hankered for a Bonapartist form of rule, frequently resorted to public referenda. Such referenda were permitted under Article 11 of the 1958 Constitution on issues concerning 'the organisation of the public authorities' and for 'the approval of a Community agreement' and 'ratification of a treaty'. They were also allowed, under Article 89, for the approval of motions of constitutional change which had been carried by the two chambers of parliament but had fallen short of a 60% joint majority. Under de Gaulle, however, referenda were held in an extra-constitutional manner, being used as plebiscitary tests of his public support. He held four referenda during the years between 1961-69, two of which concerned constitutional matters which should first have been presented to parliament for its approval. De Gaulle's defeat, however, in the 1969 referendum and the low turnout achieved by President Pompidou for his 1972 referendum has persuaded succeeding French Presidents to be more careful in their use of this weapon of direct democracy.

TABLE 2 : REFERENDA DURING THE FIFTH REPUBLIC

DATE		ISSUE	TURNOUT	VOTES IN FAVOUR
Sept	1958	New constitution	85%	79%
Jan	1961	Self-determination for Algeria	77%	75%
Apr	1962	Algeria's independence	76%	91%
Oct	1962	Direct election of the President	77%	62%
Apr	1969	Reform of the Senate and regions	81%	47%
Apr	1972	Enlargement of the EEC	60%	68%

During the years between 1958 and 1986 the agents of the President's executive power have been the Prime Minister and his team of cabinet ministers. The Prime Minister's principal task has been to manage the majority coalition in the National Assembly and ensure that presidential policy is successfully steered through parliament. He is supported in this work by a private office staff of around 30 advisers at the Hôtel Matignon.[1] In theory, the French Prime Minister's powers are extensive and comparable in many respects to that of his British counterpart. According to Article 21 of the Constitution, he is in charge of directing 'the operation of government', is responsible for national defence and has the right to appoint and dismiss ministers and senior administrative and military officers. These powers were usurped, however, by Presidents de Gaulle, Pompidou, Giscard d'Estaing and Mitterrand. This forced the Fifth Republic's first nine Prime Ministers (see Table 3) to play a more humble managerial role, taking charge of day-to-day rather than strategic affairs. They became subject to sudden dismissal as soon as they lost favour with the President, for example, Georges Pompidou in July 1968 and Pierre Mauroy in July 1984, and were similarly imperilled if they attempted to outshine the

---

[1] Such private ministerial offices, which are staffed by personally selected, politically sympathetic civil servants, are termed, confusingly, *cabinets*.

head of state, as Jacques Chirac discovered in August 1976. Only with the March 1986 National Assembly elections, returning a majority party to the legislature opposed to the presidential coalition, have the tables been turned. The President has been forced to accept a Prime Minister and cabinet from the opposition coalition and the Prime Minister, Jacques Chirac, has made full claim to the executive powers set out in Article 21, reducing the President to a backstage arbiter role.

TABLE 3 : PRIME MINISTERS IN THE FIFTH REPUBLIC, 1958-86

	PARTY	TERM
Michel Debré	UNR (RPR)	Jan 1959 — Apr 1962
Georges Pompidou	UNR (RPR)	Apr 1962 — June 1968
Maurice Couve de Murville	UDR (RPR)	July 1968 — June 1969
Jacques Chaban-Delmas	UDR (RPR)	June 1969 — July 1972
Pierre Messmer	UDR (RPR)	July 1972 — May 1974
Jacques Chirac	UDR (RPR)	May 1974 — Aug 1976
Raymond Barre	UDF	Aug 1976 — May 1981
Pierre Mauroy	Socialist	May 1981 — July 1984
Laurent Fabius	Socialist	July 1984 — Mar 1986
Jacques Chirac	RPR	Mar 1986 —

French ministerial cabinets have resembled more the American rather than the British model as a result of Article 23 of the constitution. This, the 'incompatibility clause', forbids cabinet ministers from holding a seat in parliament. It was devised to prevent the unscrupulous scramble for ministerial office that had characterised the Third and Fourth Republics and to dissuade ministers from retiring early. In practice, it has served to weaken ties with parliament and foster a specialised form of cabinet government. Presidents and Prime Ministers appoint both party politicians and technical and administrative experts to ministerial rank. These ministers concentrate upon their own departmental work, developing close relationships with civil servants and interest group representatives and being served by small advisory teams (*cabinets*) of their own. Policy is made primarily through small groups (*conseils restreints*) composed of interested departmental ministers, the Prime Minister and President in meetings which are held at the Élysée Palace. French cabinets thus lack the collectivity of the British model, with the full, 40-member Council of Ministers acting primarily as a rubber-stamping body. They are usually dominated by the President, but the Prime Minister and individual ministers can have a significant influence on the final details of policies, particularly in areas which have little interest for the head of state.

Organs of Control

Legislative The powers of individual and opposition members of the legislature have been deliberately weakened by the constitution of the Fifth Republic in an effort to foster firm and stable executive government.

The legislative authority of parliament has, in particular, been reduced. Parliament in the Fifth Republic is only allowed, according to Article 34, to pass laws in a restricted 'domain' (incorporating areas such as taxation, civil rights, electoral laws and penal matters) and to lay down general guidelines in the areas of education, labour law, local government and social security. In spheres outside this domain the government is left to legislate by decree and even for subjects inside the 'parliamentary domain' the legislature can delegate power to the administration to rule by ordinances (countersigned by the President) for a specified period.

Inside parliament, the 19 specialised standing committees which considered bills during the Fourth Republic have been reduced to six (the 61-member defence, foreign affairs, finance and legal/administrative affairs committees and the 121-member cultural/social affairs and economic affairs committees) and the government's control over committee chairs and the parliamentary agenda has been strengthened. Full-scale debates are infrequent, the number of censure motions permitted is severely restricted, few private members' bills are approved, and the opposition, contrary to British practice, has no right to parliamentary time of its own.

In addition, the government is now able to force through legislation with little debate as a result of the Fifth Republic's constitutional rules. Article 47 of the constitution, designed to ensure that the government has revenue funds, stipulates that parliament has only 70 days to debate and vote on the annual budget. Once this period has elapsed the government is permitted to impose the measure by ordinance. For other bills, the government can employ 'guillotine' procedures, pledging its 'responsibility', and can insist on a single vote on the full text (*vote bloqué*) without accepting any floor amendments. The resort to such expedients can damage the standing of an administration, but is frequently necessary as a result of the pressure on parliamentary time imposed by Article 28, which restricts the parliamentary year to one of only 170 days distributed in two sessions between October-December and April-June. Outside of this period the government is empowered to rule by decree.

These constitutional rules have significantly increased the authority of the executive during the Fifth Republic, but have by no means fully expunged the influence of parliament and its deputies and senators. It is still vital for the Prime Minister to command Assembly majorities. Deputies can thus force policy changes by threats of a revolt: this was particularly evident during the Giscard presidency when the majority coalition was internally divided. Deputies can also make useful amendments to bills which are accepted by the government and can seek to influence outside public opinion through speeches in debates and during weekly 'question time' (*questions d'actualité*), as well as acting as scrutinising watchdogs through their work on standing committees and ad hoc inquiry committees.

The directly elected 577-member National Assembly remains the dominant chamber in the Fifth Republic parliament.[1] It examines the budget first, its members are in a position to overthrow the government on a censure or confidence motion, and it can override bills vetoed by the Senate. The Senate upper chamber does, however, act as a partial and sometimes salutary check on the executive and the lower chamber. Its 319 members (296 from metropolitan France, 13 from France's overseas départements and territories and 10 representing French nationals abroad) are elected indirectly, a third at a time every three years, at the département level by an electoral college composed of members of the National Assembly and delegates from département and municipal councils. They serve nine-year terms. This system of election gives a

---

[1]   555 of the National Assembly's deputies are drawn from metropolitan France, 22 from France's overseas départements and territories (See Appendix C). In the 1986 National Assembly election, deputies were elected from party lists in multi-member seats at the département level by proportional representation. In previous elections they were elected in single-member constituencies by the two-ballot 'run-off' system, with a 12.5% second round cut-off threshold. This electoral system has been restored by the new Prime Minister, Jacques Chirac.

bias to small commune and rural areas and means that the Senate is still a bastion for the independent-minded, and often Centre Party, politicians who dominated the Third and Fourth Republics. It has thus acted as an irritant for Presidents from both the Right and Left, encouraging de Gaulle to attempt to change its method of selection in 1969. Legislation vetoed by the Senate is usually taken to a joint conciliation conference of the two chambers at which a compromise solution is accepted. On other occasions the Senate's veto is overridden by a 'definitive vote' of the National Assembly or its suggested amendments are upheld by the government which has been given time to reflect and reconsider.

Judicial The nine-member Constitutional Council forms an important judicial watchdog to ensure that legislation passed by parliament conforms to the constitution. The Council's members, who serve non-renewable nine-year terms, are chosen three at a time at triennial intervals, a third each being appointed by the President of the Republic, the President of the Senate and the President of the National Assembly. It is obliged to rule on 'organic laws' and parliamentary procedure and establish the correct balance between the executive and legislature spheres of government. It will also examine legislation on the request of the President, Prime Minister, the President of either chamber of parliament and, since 1974, that of 60 deputies or senators, with its decisions being binding. The Council was, until 1970, regarded as firmly under the government's tutelage, controversially declining to rule, for example, in 1962 on de Gaulle's referendum to change the constitution. Since 1970, however, it has begun to act with greater independence, forcing a series of important modifications to government legislation. The Council was, as a result of past selections, until recently a predominantly conservative body. This caused serious problems for the Mitterrand administration as it attempted to push through its nationalisation and decentralisation reforms in 1981-82.[1]

A second and older judicial review body is the prestigious *Conseil d'État* (Council of State). It acts as a final court of appeal for administrative cases and, staffed by senior civil servants, gives advice to government on bills submitted and on constitutional

---

[1] During the 1981-86 Mitterrand administration the Council reviewed 76 laws, rejecting 3 outright and forcing major alterations to 31. Since March 1986 it has forced significant changes to the Chirac government's proposed privatisation and newspaper reform acts.

matters. It has a tradition for upholding the rights of the individual against the State, defending republican traditions and being willing to involve itself in constitutional controversies. However, its decisions are not binding, as was displayed graphically in 1962 and 1969 when its declaration that de Gaulle had acted unconstitutionally in calling referenda was ignored by the executive.

Both the Constitutional Council and Conseil d'État function today as important judicial watchdogs and can significantly influence public opinion, forcing the executive to reconsider controversial decisions. However, they lack the influence and independent review powers of the American Supreme Court or the Italian and West German Federal Constitutional Courts. The problem for both bodies remains Article 5 of the 1958 constitution which has made the President the ultimate arbiter and guardian of the constitution. This has enabled a firm-minded President to ride roughshod over two councils, as de Gaulle succeeded in doing in 1962 and 1969.

Central and Local Government Relations

A strong executive supported by a powerful administrative machine has emerged during the Fifth Republic. It wields considerable patronage influence over a wide range of publicly controlled institutions ranging from the nationalised industries to the broadcasting medium. The central executive also penetrates into the provinces, exerting considerable authority in the sphere of local government.

France, despite its size and regional diversity and vitality[1], has long been a unitary state ruled from the centre. Successive governments have always feared weakening the centre's grip over the provinces in case secessionist tendencies, which remain latent in regions such as Brittany and Corsica, became unmanageable. More than 400 *prefects* were thus appointed by the central administration to oversee the implementation of government policies, maintain law and order and keep an eye on local expenditure in each of the country's 22 regions, 96 *départements*,

[1]   The strength and importance of the French provincial press is the most striking indicator of such regional vitality.

320 *arrondissements*, 3530 *cantons* and 36 000 *communes* during the years between 1958 and 1982.

The *prefect* functioned as a powerful political figure, dominating his locality in the manner of an imperial governor or district commissioner. He worked primarily at the département level of the local government system, being head of the locally elected *conseil général* and dominating it through the system of *tutelle* (supervision and control). Below him was an elected network of more than 36 000 commune councils (*conseils municipaux*), headed by mayors and comprising 465 000 local councillors, which were concerned with implementing policies and with local roads and housing. This local government machine was impressive in its size and the numbers of elected personnel involved, but in reality its officers enjoyed only limited powers.[1] This resulted from the severe restrictions which were placed on the fund-raising discretion of local councils and the removal of key policy sectors, such as education and the police, from their purview.[2] However, while French local councils were unusually dependent upon the centre for funding and were dominated by their assigned prefects, they were never totally powerless as a result of the composition of their elected officeholders. Many mayors and département councillors, as a result of the system of *cumul des mandats*, were also influential National Assembly senators or deputies or even government civil servants or ministers and were able to employ their influence at the centre to exert favours from prefects to the benefit of their localities.[3]

Changes began to be made to this local government system from the late 1960s as a result of a growing public desire for a greater

---

[1] In England, Scotland and Wales, by comparison, there are 9000 parish and county councils and 96 000 councillors.

[2] In the mid 1970s French local authorities received half their funds from the centre, while local taxes accounted for only 18% of all state revenue collected and local spending 13% of total public expenditure. In West Germany, by contrast, where decentralisation was far more advanced, local authorities were responsible for half of total government spending and received only a quarter of their income from the centre.

[3] Such multiple office-holding was encouraged by the brevity of the French parliamentary year. Limitations on the cumul des mandats have, however, recently been imposed by legislation passed in December 1985 by a joint session of the National Assembly and Senate which limits deputies and senators to a maximum of one other official elective office and forbids any one person combining the presidency of both a regional and a département council.

devolution of decision-making authority to render government less remote and more efficient. President Pompidou, in response, introduced an additional, third, upper advisory and co-ordinating layer of 22 regional councils and economic and social committees in 1973. These bodies were composed of each region's parliamentary deputies and senators, delegates from département councils and representatives of local interest groups, with a centrally appointed prefect as their executive officer. The socialist Mitterrand administration went a radical step further in 1982 by allowing for the direct election of regional councillors and by turning the council's elected chairman into the chief executive officer for the region. This transformed the prefect into a mere administrative agent under the title *Commissaire de la République* (commissioner). In addition, the regions and local authorities have been granted greater tax-raising and policy-making powers of their own and there has also been a growing tendency for them to draw their funds from the centre in the form of generalised 'block grants' rather than specified project grants. These reforms have done something to redress the unequal balance between the centre and localities. They represent part of a continuing liberalising and democratising process that has been evident in the French polity during the last decade, embracing judicial, parliamentary and administrative reform. Still, however, the French polity today remains unusually centralised and under the dominance of its large and skilled administrative machine.

The Party System in the Fifth Republic

Political parties provide the bridge between people and government, channeling popular demands and interests into practical policies. They act, in addition, as institutions of mobilisation and integration and reflect in their strength, organisation, number and size the nature of the surrounding society.

The relative backwardness and fragmentation of the French economy and society during the 1950s gave rise to an unusually complex and divisive multi-party system. In 1956, for example, 18 political groupings competed in the parliamentary election, twelve of which succeeded in gaining representation in the National Assembly. A significant number of these were centrist 'political clubs' orientated towards local rural and small town constituency level needs. Party organisation was also rudimentary, with France lacking the disciplined and well organised party structures to be found across the English Channel.

During the three decades since 1956, however, significant changes have been evident in the French party system, which has become streamlined and simplified and more professional in structure.[1] Four to five main party groupings have now emerged, consistently capturing over 90% of the national vote, with two broader, informal coalitions of the Left and Right now contesting for presidential power and parliamentary dominance. These changes have been brought about both by the new institutions of the Fifth Republic and by the changing social temper of contemporary France.

The switch to single-member constituencies and the two-ballot majority system encouraged the emergence of informal electoral pacts among Right, Left and Centrist parties, in the form of seat apportioning agreements or stand-down 'primary agreements'.[2] This process was given further stimulus in the Fifth Republic by the strengthening of the executive organs, which raised the stakes for victory and defeat in electoral contests. In particular, the emergence of the directly elected President as the dominant political institution forced the creation of presidential party coalitions in the same manner as the broadly based 'catch-all' Democrat and Republican coalitions in the United States. In France, these presidential coalitions took on an ideological character, reflecting the historic Left-Right divide that has characterised French politics ever since the 1789 revolution.

However, while the new institutions of the Fifth Republic have served to encourage a simplification and bipolarisation of the French party system, economic and social changes have possibly been of even greater importance. The last three decades have been ones of unprecedented growth and modernisation for the French economy. There has been a significant shift from the land and agriculture towards larger-scale industry and urban professional and service occupations. The proportion of the workforce employed in agriculture has fallen, for example, from 25% of the total in 1956 to scarcely 7% today, with urbanisation levels rising

---

[1] Still today, however, fewer than 2% of France's registered voters belong to political parties. This compares with a figure of 4-5% in West Germany and Britain.

[2] Under the latter system, which has been particularly favoured by the Left Coalition, candidates from all parties within a coalition contest the first ballot before standing down in favour of the best placed candidate for the crucial second ballot.

from 60% to 80% of the total. This, combined with the spread of modern motor and televisual communications systems, has reduced the parochialism of French society and bred a more national and modernistic political culture. The ideological fissures in French society have also noticeably lessened as the previously divisive issues of the monarchy, the colonies and state-church relations have been largely resolved, enabling attention to be focused increasingly on the bread-and-butter economic issues which typify politics in other West European states.[1]

French politics today is dominated by four parties — the RPR Gaullists, the UDF Giscardians, the Socialist Party and the Communist Party, grouped into two loose and uneasy Right and Left coalitions. One extremist 'flash party', Jean Marie Le Pen's National Front, has, in addition, emerged in recent years.

The Coalition of the Right[2] The parties of the Right were traditionally supporters of the monarchy and the established church, and favoured governance by a privileged élite. They have over the years come to accept the idea of a republican and secular society, but still favour firm, central elitist rule and have become strong supporters of a market economy in which individual enterprise is properly rewarded. The parties of the Right frequently found themselves excluded from government during the centrist-dominated Third and Fourth Republics, but dominated politics at the presidential and parliamentary levels during the first 23 years of the Fifth Republic (see Table 4).

The principal party of the Right during this period was the *Gaullist Party*. This party had its roots in the extremist, anti-party *Rassemblement* (Rally) *du Peuple Français (RPF)* established by General de Gaulle in 1947 in opposition to the Fourth Republic political system: a loosely organised 'flash party' which attracted one million members at its peak, but which rapidly lost support and was disbanded in 1953. When de Gaulle assumed the presidency in 1958 he established, despite his distaste for party politics, a new and better organised party body, the *Union pour la Nouvelle République (UNR)*. This swiftly grew in popularity from a national support level of 20% in 1958 to one of 44% in 1968 and became the

---

[1] France is now a largely secular society. The church-state link was severed in 1905 and, although 80% of the population nominally describe themselves as Catholics, barely 15% are regular church attenders.

[2] The terms 'Right' and 'Left' have their origin in the seating positions adopted in the National Assembly during the French Revolution of 1789.

TABLE 4 : NATIONAL ASSEMBLY ELECTION RESULTS, 1958-1986

% OF VOTES (First Ballot)

	Far Left	PCF	Socialists and MRG	Centre Parties	RP/CDS UDF	Gaullists RPR (UDR)	Far Right
Oct 1958	—	19%	16%	42%	—	20%	3%
Nov 1962	2%	22%	13%	25%	6%	32%	1%
Mar 1967	2%	23%	19%	13%	6%	35%	1%
June 1968	5%	21%	17%	11%	5%	38%	2%
Mar 1973	4%	21%	21%	13%	11%	27%	3%
Mar 1978	3%	21%	25%	—	20%	22%	3%
June 1981	1%	16%	38%	—	19%	21%	3%
Mar 1986	1%	10%	32%	—		44%	10%

SEAT DISTRIBUTION (Metropolitan France)

	Far Left	PCF	Socialists and MRG	Centre Parties	RP/CDS UDF	Gaullists RPR (UDR)	Other Right
Oct 1958	—	10	44	213	—	198	—
Nov 1962	2	41	65	106	20	229	2
Mar 1967	4	72	116	40	40	190	8
June 1968	—	33	57	31	60	282	7
Mar 1973	1	73	102	32	82	173	11
Mar 1978	—	86	112	—	119	145	12
June 1981	—	44	286	—	61	83	—
Mar 1986[1]	—	35	216	—	129	148	49[2]

[1] Includes overseas seats
[2] 35 National Front, 14 'Other Right'

largest single party in the National Assembly, gaining a disproportionate share of parliamentary seats as a result of the workings of the French electoral system.[1] The UNR (renamed the *Union des Démocrates pour la République (UDR)* in 1968) was typical of French political parties in being highly personalised, being formed by and depending heavily upon the charismatic personality of its leader. Its political philosophy represented, at first, a curious mix between principles of the Right and Left. It was,

[1] The UNR Gaullists were significantly weaker at the local government and Senate level.

for example, strongly nationalistic and anti-American in its foreign policy stance, but favoured a statist and protectionist economic policy at home. This gained the Gaullists early support from a broad cross-section of society, including industrial workers.

The domination of the UDR by its leader meant, however, that it underwent serious decline once de Gaulle retired from the presidency and politics in 1969. It began to be challenged in the 'Right Coalition' by the *Independent Republican Party (RP)* which had been founded in 1962 by the then Finance Minister, Valéry Giscard d'Estaing, bringing together a group of centrist 'political clubs'. The RP projected itself as a moderate centre-right party committed to the European ideal, improved relations with America, the introduction of liberalising and decentralising social and administrative reforms, and a 'social market economy' approach to economic affairs, combining economic liberalism with selective state intervention on the grounds of social justice. It was a weakly organised parliamentary faction but grew in strength with the political advance of its leader during the 1970s. When Giscard assumed the presidency in 1974, he set about organising the formation of a new broadly based, mass membership centre-right coalition which would include other centrist groups which had been squeezed by the bipolarisation of politics during the Fifth Republic. The *Union pour la Démocratie Française (UDF)* umbrella coalition was thus formed in February 1978, comprising the Republican Party, the *Radical Party* and the *Centre des Démocrates Sociaux (CDS)*. It captured 20% of the vote at the National Assembly election of March 1978 and rapidly boasted a membership of 300 000 and deepening roots at the local government level.[1]

The Gaullist party responded to the challenge from the RP and UDF during the 1970s by overhauling its organisation and revamping its image under the leadership of Jacques Chirac, who renamed the party the *Rassemblement pour la République (RPR)* in December 1976. Its membership grew to over 700 000 and federations were established throughout the nation's 96 départements. The party failed to recapture its dominance of the 1958-68 period, but managed to maintain itself as the largest single party in the splintered Right Coalition. In the process, it shifted further to the right in complexion and outlook. The Gaullist RPR under Chirac remained fiercely nationalistic in foreign policy

[1]   It should be noted that French party terms such as 'radical' do not correspond to their English meaning: French 'radicals' are in fact moderates or centrists.

outlook, but began to oppose state intervention in economic and industrial matters.

The rightward shift in the economic policies of the parties of the Right Coalition meant that the social and geographical bases of their support became more clearly defined than was evident during the de Gaulle era. Strong support was received from middle-class groups, rural areas, Catholic churchgoers, the elderly and women. Significant sections of the popular press, particularly Robert Hersant's *Le Figaro, France-Soir, L'Aurore, Le Parisien Libéré* national and provincial newspaper empire and, recently, Sir James Goldsmith's *L'Express*, have given intellectual support to the Right Coalition parties. The Right Coalition has customarily enjoyed a 55:45 majority within what has been seen as a naturally conservative French society, but in recent years they have found themselves challenged by the Coalition of the Left.

The Coalition of the Left The parties of the Left trace their roots to their early support for the French Revolution and the egalitarian republican ideal. During the 19th century they opposed the privileges of the monarchic and aristocratic élite and pressed for a separation of church and state. These aims were achieved during the Third Republic. In more recent years politicians on the Left have pressed for greater popular participation and control and have favoured an interventionist government economic strategy.

The progenitors of the contemporary Left were the Radical Republicans of the 19th century. A fully-fledged *Socialist Party* was subsequently created by Jean Jaures in 1905 in response to industrial and urban development. The party held more than 20% of the French National Assembly seats in 1914 but became internally divided between revolutionary, centrist and reformist wings, splitting in two at the Tours Congress of 1920. Revolutionary socialists, who had been impressed by the Bolshevik revolution of 1917, established a strong, authoritarian and centrally organised *French Communist Party (PCF)* closely linked to Moscow. The rump of more moderate socialists remained in place under the label the *Section Française de l'Internationale Ouvrière (SFIO)* under the leadership of Léon Blum. The two parties of the Left were to be only temporarily reconciled in the succeeding half century during the Moscow-supported Popular Front period of 1934-36 and the resistance period of 1941-45.

The Communist Party established itself during the years between 1920 and 1947 as one of the strongest and certainly the best organised parties in France. It attracted the support of over 20% of the French electorate in response to its virulent opposition to fascism during the 1930s and early 1940s and its resistance activities, and by 1945 it boasted a membership of one million, distributed through a widespread network of factory and local 'cells' leading up to a controlling Central Committee and Politburo. The party has experienced decline, however, since 1947. Its close connections with Moscow forfeited it considerable support during the 'cold war' era of the 1950s and 1960s and forced it into a parliamentary ghetto. At the same time the PCF acted as a surprisingly conservative force during these decades, despite its rhetorical espousal of workers' revolution. It gave tacit support to General de Gaulle during the 1960s, as a result of his independent, anti-American foreign policy stance, and it failed to play a revolutionary role during the 1968 'Paris disturbances'.

The party attempted to adopt a somewhat more reformist and independent line during the détente era of the 1970s, espousing its attachment to democratic procedures, revamping its internal organisation and entering into a 'common programme' with the Socialists in 1972. However, this alliance proved to be a mistake for the PCF and had to be abruptly severed in 1977. It resulted in a transfer of support to the Socialist Party and a decline in the PCF's national vote to a low of 10% in 1986 and party membership to below 450 000. The Communist Party remained a force in the northern industrial belt and the Paris inner suburbs and retained the mayorships of many urban areas, carefully attending to the welfare of its constituents. It also enjoyed the support of the powerful *Confédération Générale du Travail (CGT)* trade union and *L'Humanité* newspaper. On the national stage, however, it was becoming increasingly marginalised. Its bases of industrial working-class support were eroded between 1979-86 by recession and secular economic and social change, threatening the PCF with irreversible decline as a political force.

The Socialist Party had been the minor party on the French Left during the period between 1930 and 1970, but had been accepted into French governments during the Third and Fourth Republics and boasted strong bases in local government. The party drew its support from middle-class white-collar groups, from the industrial areas of the Central Nord and Paris suburbs and from poor, rural small farming areas of the south-east and south-west, including Protestant tracts of Languedoc. During the 1950s and 1960s the SFIO, under the leadership of Guy Mollet, moved progressively towards the centre in its policy approach, but its electoral support declined alarmingly from a figure of 23% in 1946 to one of only 8% in 1968, with membership at the latter date numbering only 70 000. This slump in its fortunes and its exclusion from government during the Fifth Republic resulted in a dramatic overhaul of the SFIO machine by Alain Savary in 1969. The party was renamed the Socialist Party (PS) and had adopted by 1971, under the leadership of François Mitterrand a more radical, left-wing policy programme favouring the extension of the public sector, workers' control and economic and administrative decentralisation. Mitterrand also sought to bring to an end the disunity of the Left which had led to its exclusion from office since 1958. He persuaded the PCF to agree to a 'Common Programme' for government and attracted to his banner, *L'Union de la Gauche*, members from the ultra-leftist *Parti Socialiste Unifié (PSU)* and from Mitterrand's own *Convention des Institutions Républicaines (CIR)*, as well as left-wing Gaullists and breakaway groups from the centrist Radical Party who had formed the *Mouvement des Radicaux de Gauche (MRG)*.

Mitterrand's unification strategy paid off for the Socialist Party. He came within a whisker of defeating Giscard d'Estaing in the 1974 presidential election, made substantial gains in the 1978 parliamentary elections, even after the PCF had severed its electoral alliance, and finally captured the presidency in 1981. The Socialist Party succeeded in attracting many former Communist blue-collar voters to its ranks and emerged as the largest single party in the National Assembly after the 1981 election. It boasted a membership of more than 200 000, the support of the *Confédération Française Démocratique du Travail (CFDT)* and *Fédération de l'Éducation Nationale (FEN)* trade unions and found many of its views reflected in the *Le Monde*, *Le Matin* and *Libération* newspapers, as well as in the weekly *Le Nouvel Observateur*. The Socialist Party had thus established itself as the major and the most broad-based party on the Left in what was a new and simplified party system.

During its period in government since 1981 the leadership of the Socialist Party has shifted increasingly towards the middle-ground in a 'social democratic' manner, enabling the French party system to begin to resemble more closely the West German model. However, there exist significant divisions and factions within the Socialist Party grouped around prominent political figures. The centre-left mainstream is led by François Mitterrand and includes his former prime ministers Laurent Fabius and Pierre Mauroy and accounts for approximately half of the party's strength. On the traditional left of the party is a faction grouped arounf party General Secretary Lionel

Jospin, with further to its left Jean-Pierre Chevènement's *Tribunite CERES* faction (Centre for Socialist Studies Research and Education), now known as the Socialism and Republic group. The other significant grouping within the party, accounting for approximately a quarter of its strength, is led by the decentralising 'social democrat' Michel Rocard. Each faction is represented on the party's ruling Executive Committee and National Secretariat through an internal system of proportional representation.

The emergence of the Socialist Party as the dominant party on the left and the establishment of the UDF and RPR as parties of the centre-right and right during the last decade have suggested that French politics is slowly moving towards a more settled two–three party system of the kind found in neighbouring West European countries. However, the mismatch between the presidential and parliamentary terms and the executive system of diarchy present serious problems for a smooth transition between different party governments, while most recently the right-wing extremist *National Front* has served to confuse the party system. These changes will be analysed in greater detail in the pages that follow.

Part Two

POLITICAL DEVELOPMENTS: 1974-1987

1945-1974: The Birth of a 'New France'

France emerged from the Second World War in a shattered and confused condition. Its northern and eastern provinces had experienced four years of bitter warfare and Nazi tutelage, its southern and central province had been controlled by the octogenarian Marshal Petain's collaborationist Vichy regime which was opposed by the underground Resistance. As General de Gaulle and the 'Free French' forces returned to proclaim the nation's liberation a bitter civil war appeared likely between Communists, Gaullists and Collaborationists, with France's continued existence as a unified liberal democracy seriously at risk.

France, however, responded to these challenges, maintained its unity and, helped by a new form of economic planning and management, proceeded to enjoy two decades of buoyant and unprecedented economic growth. Once the 'sick man' of Western Europe, France became one of its economic success stories with overall growth averaging 4.6% per annum during the 1950s and 5.6% during the 1960s. The country's national income per capita, which had stood at 70% of the United Kingdom level in 1945, was almost one-and-a-half times that of its northern rival in 1974. France truly entered the industrial age during these 'miracle years', with its economy and society being radically remoulded. There was tremendous spatial and occupational mobility as workers moved away from backward rural Western France towards blue and white collar employment in the burgeoning urban centres of the Eastern and Central regions of France. These years also witnessed the decline of traditional small-scale enterprises — shops, farms, workshops — and a shift to larger, salaried concerns — hyper-markets, agri-combines, factories — and the demise in customary social institutions and hierarchies. Politically, however, this period of great economic and social change proved, perhaps not surprisingly, to be one of fickle instability, with the nation lurching violently between atomistic democracy and paternalistic autocracy.

1945-1958: Laying the Foundations of the French Renaissance

Much of the credit for France's smooth return to parliamentary democracy in 1946 can be apportioned, curiously, to the inveterate opponent of party and parliamentary systems, General Charles de Gaulle. De Gaulle, placing top priority on the need to retain national order and unity, formed a broad-based transitional liberation government which included prominent Communists and proceeded to introduce a pragmatic and far-reaching series of social and economic reforms, including nationalisation of the coal, gas and electricity industries, Air France, the chief banks and the collaborationist Renault automobile works, as well as the introduction of a comprehensive system of social security and the extension of the franchise to women. These reforms helped foster a sense of reward and reconciliation in the nation, which was furthered by the rapid, but controlled, purge of Vichy collaborators.

De Gaulle resigned as interim President, however, in January 1946 once the new Constituent Assembly had decided to reject his proposals for a strong presidential form of government in favour of a weak parliamentary system and was to remain in the political wilderness for twelve years, emerging only briefly to challenge the Fourth Republic democratic system with the launching of the anti-constitutional, neo-fascist RPF in 1947. Politics became once more a game of factional bargaining and musical chairs during the years 1946-58. However, although governmental instability during this period paralysed policy-making in areas of social and political reform, the French economy managed to prosper as a result of the efforts of French industrialists working in partnership with a new, skilled and innovative central corps of technocratic civil servants. The new system of 'indicative planning' established in 1946 by Jean

---

[1] The new system of 'indicative planning' was centred around the Planning Commissariat (*Commissariat au Plan*), a small but expert 60-member body of professional civil servants, which, working in consultation with other government departments, established committees of industrialists, trade unionists and academic experts to discuss and frame five-year plans 'indicating' future economic and social priorities and assessing probable forthcoming economic trends.

Monnet and the creation of the European Coal and Steel Company (ECSC) in 1952 and the European Economic Community in 1958 provided a conducive framework within which French industry could expand. Diplomatically, the Fourth Republic years also saw France re-emerge on the international stage as a partner in the new NATO defence alliance and to begin to take steps towards decolonisation with the granting of independence to Indo-China (1954) and Morocco and Tunisia (1956).

1958-1969: The De Gaulle Era

The Fourth Republic, although outwardly successful, lacked deep popular affection. It proved to be easily toppled in May 1958 by an army revolt at the height of the Algerian crisis, bringing General de Gaulle back into power after an interval of twelve years. De Gaulle's second assumption of power differed markedly, however, from the circumstances of 1945/6. It was opposed by the French Left, who saw May 1958 as an unconstitutional right-wing coup. Secondly, de Gaulle was not to retire rapidly once the immediate Algerian crisis had been solved. He was, instead, to remain as head of state for eleven years and, in the process, to refashion radically the French constitution.

The early years of the de Gaulle era were ones of tension and threatened instability as the Algerian issue continued to dominate the French political scene. De Gaulle faced constant threats on his life from OAS extremists.[1] De Gaulle used this instability to establish a strongly personalised and autocratic system of government based on the use of plebiscitary referenda. Such a system of rule suited a man who was, by temperament, aloof, arrogant and domineering, and who, being drawn from the French military service-aristocracy, was more used to giving direct orders than to party political bargaining. De Gaulle gained the support of his UNR party colleagues for this presidentialist strategy, thus institutionalising the *de facto* dominance of the President over the Prime Minister in the new Fifth Republic political system.

---

[1] *Organisation de l'Armée Secrète*, a terrorist organisation formed in 1961 and headed by Raoul Salam (imprisoned 1962-68) which sought to overthrow the Algerian government and re-establish *Algérie française*.

De Gaulle used his new power most visibly in the sphere of foreign affairs where he set France on a unique new unilateralist course, withdrawing France from the integrated military command structure of NATO in 1966 and establishing the nation as a powerful 'Third Front' straddled between the two superpowers with its own independent nuclear arsenal (the *force de frappe*). De Gaulle also, pragmatically, speeded up the process of decolonisation in Francophone Africa, negotiating Algeria's independence in 1962, while at the same time making sure that France's economic links with her former colonies were maintained. He also, most importantly, purged the French army of its extremist elements and brought it firmly under political control. In the domestic economic sphere, de Gaulle displayed less interest, delegating decision-making to his Prime Ministers and Finance Ministers. He gave broad support, however, to an active and interventionary role for the state in strategic sectors of the economy and provided a decade of political stability for the country's technocrats and industrialists.

The de Gaulle years were in many respects ones of striking success for France both at home and overseas. The rate of economic growth accelerated, with gross national product per capita almost doubling between 1960 and 1970, (taking it above the UK level). A 'New France', urbanised, industrialised, younger, better educated and less hidebound by tradition, began to emerge. The pace of political and institutional change proved, however, to be far slower, with de Gaulle continuing to rule in an intrusive, centralised, paternalistic manner. This created a dangerously widening disjuncture between the French economic base and the political structure.

The 'Events' of May 1968 and their Aftermath

The emergence of opposition to the Gaullist state first became evident in the presidential election of 1965 when François Mitterrand, the last-minute candidate of the Left, made a surprisingly strong second ballot challenge. Two years later, the swing away from the government was underlined by the UNR's loss of its absolute Assembly majority in the elections of March 1967. A year later the de Gaulle government and the Fifth Republic political system came close to being swept away by an anarchic tide of unrest which became known as the *May Events*. A complex mix of forces, both new and old, precipitated these disturbances which shook the French body politic. In the short term, this attempted 'revolution' failed, but from a longer-term perspective the 'May events' heralded the end of paternalistic Gaullism and sowed the seeds for a new, more liberal and participative era in French politics.

Four short-term factors and events brought opposition to the de Gaulle administration to a head in May 1968. Firstly, the decision of Prime Minister Pompidou to legislate by decree in the economic and social sphere for six months, following the UNR's loss of its absolute majority in March 1967. Secondly, a sudden downturn in the economy, the first of the post-war era, which sent unemployment up to 450 000 and led to a sharp rise in the inflation rate, which the government attempted to counter by a policy of fiscal and wage austerity. Thirdly, the outbreak of student unrest on France's rapidly expanding university campuses in protest against inadequate conditions and outdated curricula and under the outside influence of the growing anti-Vietnam War movement and the radical new Chinese 'Cultural Revolution'. Fourthly, plans to hold demonstrations by left-wing groups anxious to mark the tenth anniversary of de Gaulle's May 1958 'coup' and the opening in Paris of peace talks aimed at bringing to an end the Vietnam War.

The early fuse was lit by ultra-leftist students who began demonstrating at Nanterre in Paris in February 1968. By May these demonstrations had reached riot proportions and by the middle of the month, following activist pressure, the students had gained the support of the CGT trade union who launched a one-day general strike in Paris. This strike rapidly spread to the provinces, leading to a wave of factory sit-ins and occupations which swept across France, involving ten million workers by 29 May. Older groups, for example small shopkeepers and peasant farmers, disturbed by recent economic changes, also joined in this orgy of violence as government control over the country disintegrated. At the height of the crisis de Gaulle's nerve snapped and he fled to Baden-Baden in West Germany to discuss the possibility of resignation with his senior military commanders. However, General Jacques Massu, the commander of the French forces, persuaded de Gaulle to remain in office, while Prime Minister Pompidou negotiated an industrial truce with the CGT, involving a package of substantial wage increases, and entered into talks to resolve the campus crisis. This successfully reduced the level of protest and violence and by June order had been reimposed. De Gaulle, on the advice of Pompidou, called a snap parliamentary election to reaffirm his mandate and the UDR gained an unprecedented landslide majority.

However, although de Gaulle emerged apparently victorious from the June 1968 Assembly elections, his political judgement and authority had been seriously undermined by his handling of the 'May crisis', while a new rival and possible successor, Georges Pompidou, had established himself on the French political scene. De Gaulle, jealous of the growing popularity of his protégé, ousted Pompidou as Prime Minister in July 1968, replacing him with the loyal, but colourless, former Foreign Minister, Maurice Couve de Murville. Within ten months, however, de Gaulle had resigned the presidency following defeat in his controversial referendum for regional and Senate reform[1], and was succeeded by his estranged *dauphin*, Georges Pompidou. De Gaulle retired to write his memoirs at his country retreat at Colombey-les-Deux-Églises, before dying in November 1970 at the age of 79.

1969-1974: The Pompidou Interregnum

Georges Pompidou, a popular and nationally respected figure, comfortably won the June 1969 presidential election which followed de Gaulle's resignation, defeating the Centrist Senate leader Alain Poher on the second ballot. Having worked closely with de Gaulle for more than 20 years as his personal adviser, *chef du cabinet* and Prime Minister, Pompidou's policy programme promised to mirror closely that of his predecessor. His style of rule seemed likely, however, to be warmer and more open, reflecting Pompidou's lively and gregarious personality.

In practice, however, the Pompidou era also saw a number of important shifts in policy emphasis. Overseas, while largely adhering to de Gaulle's 'Third Force' strategy, France became somewhat more 'European' and co-operative in outlook, supporting, for example, Britain's entry into the European Community in 1973. At home, Pompidou abandoned de Gaulle's quixotic attempts to introduce radical 'new society' profit-sharing and workers' participation reforms and adopted a more 'liberal', market-orientated approach to economic affairs. In addition, the

---

[1] De Gaulle had proposed replacing the obstructionist, Centrist-dominated, Senate with a new, indirectly elected, advisory body composed of local and interest group notables.

new President, who was an *École Normale Supérieure* trained economist and former director of the Rothschild Frères merchant bank, was to take a more direct and personal interest in domestic economic affairs, making the modernisation and continued industrialisation of France his chief priority. This significantly extended the 'Presidential Sector' into an area over which future Presidents would seek to retain control.

The early record of the new Pompidou administration proved to be impressive both at home, where healthy rates of industrial growth were recorded, and abroad. From 1972, however, the Pompidou team began to lose its grip and became buffeted by events. The President called a referendum on the enlargement of the European Community in April 1972 with the aim of splitting the fledgling Socialist-Communist alliance, but was embarrassed himself by a low public turnout after a Left opposition campaign for a poll boycott. His government's popularity was further reduced by a series of scandals and by calls for greater social and administrative reform. The President belatedly began to respond to these demands in 1973 with the launch of the 'Provins Programme' and the introduction of a system of regional advisory councils. He was unable, however, to implement fully these measures, dying in April 1974 at the age of 62, after enduring the debilitating terminal illness of bone-marrow cancer.

The Pompidou interregnum had served to provide an important period of stability and to legitimise and extend the influence of the Fifth Republic presidential regime. It had also seen subtle changes of policy approach, with the shift of the UDR to a more narrowly orthodox, conservative position. Pompidou's death also, however, closed the door on the old Gaullist age and inaugurated a new political era in which a new generation of leaders would attempt to deal with the complex problems and demands of the 'New France' and to liberalise and democratise the authoritarian Gaullist system.

The May 1974 Presidential Election

President Pompidou's death in April 1974 came at an awkward time for the Right Coalition, which was undergoing a slow metamorphosis as it adjusted itself to the absence of the charismatic Charles de Gaulle. The UDR majority wing of the ruling coalition had always been a weakly organised and ideologically disparate grouping of politicians and activists, who had been controlled loosely by the former Resistance 'barons' Michel Debré, Jacques Foccart, Jacques Chaban-Delmas, Roger Frey, Olivier Guichard, Jacques Soustelle and André Malroux. They were united in their strong, independent and nationalistic approach to foreign affairs, but differed substantially on economic and social matters; some, the so-called 'Gaullist fundamentalists', favouring an interventionist, paternalist, quasi-socialist approach, others favouring free-market liberalism. In the absence of a tightly structured form of party organisation, these personal and ideological cleavages threatened to create serious problems for the UDR once the unifying figures of de Gaulle and Pompidou had departed. This is what happened in 1974.

Presidential candidates were chosen by the UDR, not by a party executive committee (Politburo), as occurred with the PCF, or by a special party Congress, as was the case with the Socialist Party, or by a series of primaries leading to a convention, as was the case in the United States, but by an informal system of *déclarations* by prominent members seeking endorsement. This system worked successfully when one obvious candidate presented himself, as in 1965 and 1969, but created chaos in 1974 when three to four indifferent personalities contested for the leadership. The first Gaullist 'notable' to throw his hat in the ring in 1974 was Jacques Chaban-Delmas (59), a former Resistance brigadier-general, National Assembly president and Prime Minister (1969-72), and the long-time Deputy for and Mayor of Bordeaux. Chaban-Delmas, however, stood on the left wing of the UDR, being a fervent believer in de Gaulle's vision of a 'new society' embracing workers' participation and regional decentralisation, while also supporting a restructuring of the social security system and a relaxation of state control over the media. Such a radical programme was opposed by conservative Gaullists. This prompted the National Assembly president Edgar Faure and Prime Minister Messmer to threaten to contest the election. Jean Royer, the mayor of Tours and minister for small shopkeepers, went one step further and tendered a firm candidature.

The Gaullist party thus put up two candidates for the 1974 presidential election, Chaban-Delmas and the maverick Jean Royer. Chaban-Delmas was viewed as the main contender and gained the greatest party backing, but large sections within the UDR, including Interior Minister Jacques Chirac and a band of 43 allies, were appalled by his domestic policy programme and transferred their support to Valéry Giscard d'Estaing, leader of the junior partner in the Right Coalition, the Independent Republicans.

Giscard (b.1926) came from a wealthy, upper-middle-class, Auvergne-based, Catholic family with distant aristocratic connections to Louis XV. His grandfather had been a prominent right-wing National Assembly deputy and his father had accumulated a fortune as an Inspector of Finance and as a director of a clutch of banking and insurance companies. Giscard himself had gained a *Croix de Guerre* for his activities with the liberation movement in 1944 and after the war enjoyed a distinguished academic career, passing through the *École Polytechnique* and the newly established *École Nationale d'Administration*. He subsequently worked for several years in the influential Ministry of Finance before being inducted into the private *cabinet* of the Finance Minister, later Prime Minister, Edgar Faure in 1953. Following this experience, Giscard decided to commit himself to a political career. He took over his grandfather's parliamentary seat for Puy-de-Dôme in 1956, and was elected into the National Assembly as a *Républicain Indépendant* at the age of 30, and built up a powerful local base as a municipal councillor in Chanonat, département councillor in Puy-de-Dôme and as the mayor of the Clermont-Ferrand suburb · of Chamalières. After first serving as a junior minister, Giscard was appointed by de Gaulle to the influential post of Finance Minister in 1962 at an unusually young age and introduced a tough anti-inflationary 'stabilisation plan'. During this period, Giscard also built up his small, but influential, *Independent Republican (IR)* party, out of a faction which broke away from the *Centre National des Indépendants et des Paysans (CNIP)* in 1962 over support for de Gaulle's constitutional referendum.

Giscard began his political career as a loyal ally of de Gaulle. However, he began publicly to voice policy differences following his dismissal as Finance Minister in 1966, establishing himself as a supporter of a freer-market approach to economic affairs and of a more 'European' and 'Atlanticist' foreign policy posture. He also, during the years between 1966 and 1969, began to reorganise the IR as a more effective political force, establishing département and regional branches and a youth wing. In April 1969 Giscard earned the undying enmity of many older Gaullists by publicly opposing the President's controversial Senate reform referendum. He maintained, however, good relations with Georges Pompidou and returned as Finance Minister in 1969-74 in a government whose policy approach was more to his liking.

Giscard had considerable success as Finance Minister during the Pompidou administration and gained a high public profile as the nation's third most important politician. This, coupled with his more conservative domestic political philosophy, his unimpeachable personal reputation and his accomplished television manner, made him a more attractive presidential candidate to a significant number of Gaullists than the flamboyant 'fundamentalist' Chaban-Delmas. Giscard was thus able to draw together a broad coalition of centre-right forces comprising old conservative Gaullists, new Chiraquian Gaullists and Centre Party supporters, led by Jean Lecanuet, the influential mayor of Rouen. This coalition was able to comfortably defeat Chaban-Delmas in the first presidential ballot on 5 May by a margin of two to one. Giscard was to face, however, a sterner challenge from the Left Coalition, whose candidate François Mitterrand had topped the First Ballot poll with a 43% share of the vote.[1]

The parties of the Left entered the 1974 presidential election race in an unusually united, amicable and optimistic mood. The Socialist Party had, following its humiliating performance in 1969 (when Gaston Defferre had captured only 5% of the presidential First Ballot vote), been revivified at the 1971 Épinay Congress by its new leader François Mitterrand. It had gained an infusion of new members, including leftist Radicals and Gaullists and defectors from the PSU; its organisation had been revamped and its leadership cadres renewed; and it had adopted a new socialist programme based around the principles of *autogestion* (workers' control), decentralisation, nationalisation, popular participation and a united-left electoral approach. This call for a new 'Popular Front' approach was reciprocated by the PCF, led since 1970 by Secretary-General Georges Marchais. Influenced by changing international events — East-West détente, the Sino-Soviet rift, and the Czech and Hungarian 'experiments' — Marchais saw the need for the PCF to strike a more independent line from Moscow in a manner akin to the Italian Communist Party. The PCF thus asserted, in 1971, its commitment to achieving the 'transition to socialism' by the democratic means of the ballot box and pledged itself, during the interim, to fighting abuses of power in the capitalist system.

An historic 'Common Programme for Government' was thus signed by the Socialist Party, MRG and PCF in June 1972, setting out a

---

[1] Giscard received 33% of the First Ballot vote, Chaban-Delmas 15% and Royer 3%. Eight other candidates stood, sharing 6% of the poll.

five-year legislative agenda for a future term of government and effecting a Second Ballot electoral agreement between the PS and PCF. This raised the credibility of the Left Coalition and paid electoral dividends in the March 1973 National Assembly elections. It led to a broadening of the base of Socialist Party support and enabled François Mitterrand to run unopposed as the 'United Left' candidate in 1974 and to top the national First Ballot poll.

Fear of a possible Second Ballot victory for the Left in 1974 had a salutary effect on the previously disunited parties in the Right Coalition. They rallied around the majority coalition's surviving candidate, Giscard d'Estaing, to provide solid support in what became the closest and most exciting presidential campaign experienced during the Fifth Republic.

Giscard, working with Jacques Hintzy (director of the Havas advertising agency), the economist Lionel Stoleru, Christian Bonnet and two former ENA graduates, Paul Mentre and Jean Serise, fought an American-style campaign with clear themes and a skilful use of the television medium. He frequently used the slogan of 'Change without Risk', promising the introduction of reforms to extend civil liberties, freedom and justice, while at the same time criticising the Left's commitment to state socialism. Giscard, casually dressed and frequently photographed with his attractive wife and four young children, projected himself as a solid family man and as a dynamic, new-style, intellectual politician who enjoyed the 'common touch'.

His opponent, François Mitterrand, was, by contrast, a ponderous and enigmatic character who excelled more at the traditional politics of public meetings than at slick television presentation and instant debate. He inducted the economists Jacques Attali and Michel Rocard into his campaign team to breathe new life into the Left Coalition's economic programme and attempted to keep his controversial PCF allies in the background. He also diluted the 1972 'Common Programme' and fought instead on a personal programme of nationalisation, decentralisation, justice, freedom, participation and social reform.

The Second Ballot campaign proved to be unusually heated with the Right Coalition constantly playing on popular fears of the dire consequences of a split mandate ('cohabitation') or the entry of Communists into the French government. As a result of such interest the turnout for polling on 18 May reached a record level of 86.7%, with the final outcome being the closest ever. Mitterrand prevailed in the départements of north-eastern, southern and south-western France and gained strong support from urban blue-collar workers and the young. Giscard was supported, in contrast, by rural north-western, eastern and central France, by middle- and upper-class groups and by the elderly. (See Table 5 and Figure 2.) This proved sufficient for a knife-edge victory of 13.4 million (50.8%) votes to 13.0 million (49.2%).

TABLE 5 : THE MAY 1974 PRESIDENTIAL ELECTION (Second Ballot)

VOTING BY SOCIAL GROUPS

	Giscard	Mitterrand
Men	46%	54%
Women	53%	47%
Age Groups		
21-34	42%	58%
35-64	50%	50%
65 and Over	60%	40%
Occupations		
Farmers	60%	40%
Professionals & Managers	74%	26%
White-Collar	50%	50%
Ordinary/ Manual	27%	73%

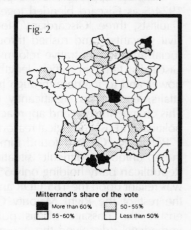

Fig. 2

Mitterrand's share of the vote

■ More than 60% ☐ 50-55%
☐ 55-60% ☐ Less than 50%

The Giscard Presidency: 1974-1981

The Giscard Style and Method of Governing

When Giscard assumed the French presidency in May 1974 he was anxious to develop a new, more modern and consensual form of presidential leadership. He sought, firstly, to project himself as an accessible and informal 'man of the people', walking to the Champs-Élysée for his inauguration ceremony, declining to wear official uniform during his monthly televised 'fireside chats' and accepting invitations to dinner at the homes of ordinary French families. Giscard, secondly, believed that the economic and social changes of the 1950s and 1960s had eroded many traditional prejudices and had created a new consensus and 'political centre'. He aimed to rule from this centre in a broad-based, coalition fashion, including in his early cabinets a significant number of Centre party politicians and inducting Socialists from the Left Opposition into bodies such as the Conseil d'État and the Economic and Social Council.[1] Giscard, thirdly, aimed to avoid the excessive interventionism displayed by Élysée staff during Pompidou's later years. Instead, he sought to concentrate on the formulation of broad policy outlines rather than on the specific details of policy implementation.

This new approach to the presidency met with early success in 1974/5 as Giscard blended together a cabinet containing five UDR Gaullists, three 'Giscardians', four Centrists and three non-political civil servants[2], and rushed through a series of popular, liberalising social and administrative reforms. It did not, however, last long. As Giscard's term in office lengthened he began to reconcentrate power and to interfere through his aides in widening areas of public affairs, ending up significantly extending the 'presidential sector'. This change in style and approach was brought about for a variety of political and psychological reasons.

Politically, Giscard found himself at the outset of his presidency in a uniquely difficult situation. With his own Independent Republican party holding only 55 seats in the National Assembly, he was reliant upon the 185 UDR and 35 Centrist deputies who made up the rest of the Right Majority Coalition to provide the support to ensure the passage of his policy programmes. He could have immediately dissolved the Assembly and called upon the public to return an increased number of IR deputies in a manner akin to that of his successor François Mitterrand in May 1981. Giscard's IR party was, however, too weakly organised to benefit from such a strategy. The President was thus forced to work with the existing balance of forces in the Right Coalition, appointing the UDR leader Jacques Chirac as his first Prime Minister. Unfortunately, however, for Giscard, Chirac was an intensely ambitious politician of diverging ideological outlook. His relations with the President became rapidly strained, leading to a damaging split in August 1976. This, in turn, soured relations between Giscard and the UDR, making it

---

[1] A body of representatives from economic interest groups which is consulted by the government to give advice on bills and debate Five-Year Plans.

[2] The key figures in this cabinet were the Giscardian Interior Minister, Michel Poniatowski, the Centrist Justice Minister, Jean Lecanuet, and the bureaucrat Foreign and Finance Ministers, Jean Sauvagnargues and Michel Fourcade.

difficult for the President to force through many of his cherished social and administrative reforms. During his final years in office Giscard thus became an increasingly isolated, chagrined and distrustful figure, who turned inwards for support to his palace guard of staff assistants and loyal bureaucrat ministers to exert control over the government machine.

Psychologially, Giscard was not by nature the common, casual and detached 'man of the people' he attempted to present himself as in 1974 and 1975. He was in fact a rational, refined, patrician personality and a trained administrator with a wide-ranging interest in economic, foreign and social policy issues. These extensive interests led him to intervene to an unusual degree in day-to-day political affairs and necessitated his establishment of a large and powerful 'general staff' team. This team was led by the general-secretaries Jean François-Poncet (1974-76), Claude-Pierre Brossolette (1976-78) and Jacques Wahl (1978-81) and the political assistants Jean Riolacci and Jean Serise and included 16 (later 27) technical advisers who oversaw the work of ministerial cabinets and who prepared the President with short policy briefs to take in to the important *Conseils restreints*. Giscard, in addition, appointed individual experts to make direct reports on controversial areas of reform — for example the Guichard report on local government reform in 1976 and the Sudreau report on workers' rights — and took a great personal interest in overseeing appointments to junior ministerial and senior civil service and nationalised industry posts. During his seven years as President, he established in power his own administrative élite, many of whom were fellow *énarques* (former ENA graduates), to preside over what became known as the 'Giscardian Republic'. Lacking solid political support from the National Assembly, however, Giscard continued to find it difficult to press through with many of the reforms he had contemplated in 1974. For this reason Giscard's term in office was chequered and one of great disappointment.

The Giscard Policy Programme

Giscard d'Estaing's policy outlook was a unique centrist mixture, drawing upon elements from both the Right and Left political traditions as well as a number of newly imported cosmopolitan ideas.

In his approach to foreign policy, the new President largely adhered to the post-1958 Gaullist consensus of French national independence buttressed by a powerful nuclear *force de frappe*, détente with the Soviet Union and an active French political role in Africa and the Arab world. He was, however, more European, Atlanticist and internationalist in outlook than either de Gaulle or Pompidou. Giscard was thus to press for closer policy co-ordination within the European Community and, in combination with his close and long-standing friend, the West German Chancellor Helmut Schmidt, took an active role in the creation of the new institutions of European and world economic summits.

At home, Giscard was an unashamed liberal in the social sphere who sought 'the greatest possible reconciliation between equality and liberty' and who saw the need to reform and update French state institutions to take account of recent economic and social developments. For example, he was anxious to extend the rights of women, who were now emerging as an increasingly important element in the French labour force, and the young. Giscard, moved by a sense of *noblesse oblige*, also sought to alleviate the lot of the very poor on the grounds of social justice. He aimed to raise minimum wages and pensions, improve facilities for the disabled and housing conditions for immigrant workers. He did not seek, however, to iron out broader social and income inequalities in an egalitarian, socialist manner. Giscard, thirdly, felt that French society was mature enough to benefit from an unshackling of the paternalistic and sometimes authoritarian controls exercised by the government in broadcasting, the arts and civil affairs. He favoured a liberalisation in the censorship laws, a break-up of the state monopoly over the ORTF (*Office de la Radio-diffusion et Télévision Française*) and an extension of individual freedoms, with the aim of creating a more tolerant and pluralistic 'advanced liberal' society.

In the economic sphere, Giscard shared President Pompidou's burning desire to see a modernised France join the 'First Industrial League' occupied by Japan, the United States and West Germany. He sought to achieve this by combining technocratic, state, long-term, strategic planning with a competitive, deregulationary, freer-market approach at the micro level. He thus sought to end state support to 'lame duck' industries and to infuse greater market and price consciousness into French industry. In the fiscal sphere, he was anxious to incorporate elements of the successful 'German model' of monetary control, a stable currency, a balanced budget and controlled wage moderation.

This reform programme was diverse and ambitious and would

require substantial cross-party co-operation if it was to be fully implemented. Such co-operation failed, however, to materialise and, faced by a worsening world economic climate, Giscard was forced to trim and make major policy compromises, usually in a Gaullist direction, during what proved to be a difficult seven years in office.

The Uneasy Giscard-Chirac Alliance: 1974-1976

The first year of the Giscard presidency was marked by the hectic introduction of a series of important social reforms and by relatively harmonious relations between the President and Prime Minister Chirac and the UDR. The minimum voting age and 'age of majority' were lowered to 18 (June 1974); Françoise Giroud, a former Socialist, and Simone Veil were appointed ministers for Women and Health Affairs and proceeded to push through bills legalising abortion during the first ten weeks of pregnancy (December 1974), permitting divorce on the grounds of mutual consent and marriage breakdown (March 1975) and forbidding sex discrimination; single parent and family parent allowances were increased, as was the level of the statutory minimum wage; provision for the handicapped was improved; a large hospital and nursery construction programme was launched; and plans were made to permit retirement on a full pension at the age of 60 and to improve the provision of maternity leave.

In addition to these social reforms, the Giscard administration rapidly introduced a series of administrative reforms aimed at relaxing state cultural and political control and fostering greater pluralism. The ORTF state broadcasting system was broken down into seven separate, new state companies, the intrusive Ministry of Information dismantled, and the opposition was given greater access to the television medium; telephone tapping was curtailed; film censorship was lifted; a weekly version of 'question time' (without, however, the provision for supplementaries) was introduced into the National Assembly; and, from December 1974, groups of 60 parliamentarians were given the right to pass legislation on to the Constitutional Council for adjudication.

Taken together, these 1974/5 reforms represented an important step towards the creation of a more tolerant, liberal and open society. Many of these measures, for example the abortion bill, were, however, opposed by conservative Centrist and UDR members of the Right Coalition and were only carried as a result of support from the opposition Left. This was an ominous and vexing development for the new administration.

The new President encountered even greater difficulties in the economic sphere, as a result of adverse external factors. Giscard was unfortunate in assuming office during what, in retrospect, proved to be a watershed period for the world economy. The post-war era of buoyant economic growth, expanding trade, low inflation and stable exchange rates was suddenly brought to an end during the early 1970s as a result of fiscal difficulties in America, sharpening industrial competition from South-east Asia's NICs (newly industrialised countries) and the quadrupling of world oil prices which followed the outbreak of the 1973/4 Arab-Israeli war. From 1973 the world economy was plunged into a new, more difficult, era of volatile exchange rates, spiralling inflation, depressed international commerce and mounting unemployment. Governments and bureaucrats, France included, inured to high rates of economic growth and viewing the post-1973 economic downturn as only a temporary phenomenon, attempted to deal with its symptoms through traditional 'stop-start' fiscal measures. A tight deflationary budget was introduced by Giscard in June 1974 in an attempt to reduce inflation, then running at a level of 16%. The consequence of this was, however, a sharp rise in the unemployment level to a figure approaching one million in what became France's first year of negative economic growth since the war. In 1975 a major £2 billion public investment and tax relief reflationary package was introduced and selective intervention sanctioned to help support troubled 'lame duck' industries and provide employment for redundant workers. Such measures, which were very much Gaullist in hue, proved, however, to have only limited success in dealing with the new phenomenon of 'stagflation' (declining industrial production combined with rising inflation). During the second period of his presidential term, Giscard was to take a broader view of the contemporary recession, and to introduce a more novel, coherent and determined recovery programme.

The Giscard-Barre Team Take Charge: 1976-1978

Relations between President Giscard and Prime Minister Chirac had been initially cordial, but rapidly deteriorated in 1975 and 1976 as a result of conflicts in temperament and policy outlook.

Superficially Jacques Chirac resembled Giscard d'Estaing in many ways. Both were tall, rangy men drawn from bourgeois élite backgrounds, who had successfully passed through the exacting ENA and had enjoyed meteoric political careers. Chirac, six years the junior of Giscard, was born in 1932 the son of a Paris businessman-banker with strong links to the Limousin region. He flirted early in his life with Communism, before swinging to the Right, fighting on the side of the settlers in the Algerian war. Chirac began his professional career working in the Court of Accounts, but was then inducted into the government secretariat by Prime Minister Pompidou. Here, like Giscard, he gained a taste for power and decided to concentrate on a political career. In 1967 he gained election as a National Assembly deputy for his home Corrèze département in Central France and proceeded to build up a solid local base as département council chairman and as a member of the Limousin regional council. Chirac gained ministerial experience in 1969, serving as a junior secretary of state to Finance Minister Giscard, and was later promoted to the Agriculture and Interior Minister posts during the final years of the Pompidou administration. In these positions, he gained the reputation for immense industry, ambition and forcefulness, being nicknamed 'the bulldozer', and he impressed Pompidou, who emerged as his patron. Ideologically, Chirac presented himself as a tough-minded conservative Gaullist, who was determined to uphold France's independence in foreign affairs and to oppose closer European integration; who was unconvinced as to the need for social reform; and who favoured a modern, interventionary economic strategy.

Chirac had supported Giscard's bid for the presidency partly because he viewed Giscard as a lesser evil than the 'Left Gaullist' Chaban-Delmas, but also for less altruistic reasons, seeking to gain the prime ministership while at the same time ending the career of his chief Gaullist rival. His period as Prime Minister proved, however, to be a fractious and unhappy one. President Giscard sought to dominate Chirac and to push through social and foreign policies of which Chirac disapproved. He also aimed to weaken the Gaullist UDR and to create a new 'political centre', thus putting an end to the traditional Left-Right division in French politics. These moves were naturally opposed by Chirac, who sought himself to extend the role of the Prime Minister in French policy-making. There was thus constant friction between the two men, with Chirac criticising the President for failing to consult with him over foreign policy and before ministerial reshuffles and finding it difficult to work with

41

Centrist ministers in a coalition which he described as a 'basket of frogs jumping in different directions'.

The Giscard-Chirac conflict finally came to a head in 1976, when the UDR Gaullists, who were already seething over the President's decision in January to support the creation of a directly elected European Parliament, revolted in July over the government's new capital gains tax bill. One month later, Prime Minister Chirac ostentatiously resigned complaining that the President had not allowed him a free enough hand. This was the first resignation by a Prime Minister during the Fifth Republic and during the years ahead Chirac was to emerge as a damaging thorn in the side of President Giscard, building up his own, more personalised, Gaullist party which would frustrate Giscard's reform programme and his dream of constructing a new political centre.

President Giscard turned outside the ranks of party politicians in selecting Chirac's replacement as Prime Minister. He chose Raymond Barre (52), the avuncular, but strong-willed, former vice-president of the European Commission and Minister of Foreign Trade, a man who had made his reputation as a neo-liberal/monetarist economics professor at the Sorbonne. Barre was granted, in addition, the important Finance Ministry portfolio and told to concentrate upon fostering economic recovery. A number of additional cabinet changes were effected in August 1976 which served to further reduce the representation of UDR (now RPR) Gaullists and induct independent new technocrats.[1] This made the government more presidentialist in character, with policy formulation being engrossed by Giscard's expanding 'general staff' advisory team. However, the administration's control over the National Assembly was further weakened as RPR deputies became increasingly rebellious, though they still recoiled from supporting the opposition on censure motions.

Faced with such Assembly opposition, the Giscard administration lost much of its liberal reformist zeal and, with unemployment now exceeding one million and inflation in double figures, concentrated instead upon economic affairs.[2] Here, Raymond Barre persuaded President Giscard to adopt a new freer-

---

[1] Only 9 of the 36 senior and junior ministers in Giscard's August 1976 government were drawn from the RPR, while 12 came from outside parliament.

[2] One exception to this was Giscard's decision to restore a city council and mayor to the Paris region in 1976.

market approach to economic affairs in imitation of the successful West German model. He believed that the French economy needed an immediate period of fiscal austerity to deal with the problem of hyperinflation, but also needed to undergo a more radical, medium-term structural change in which the state departed from day-to-day price fixing and protectionist involvement in the economy and restricted its activities to long-term, strategic planning, infrastructural support and the provision of a stable fiscal environment. This would entail policies of 'rationalisation' in declining industrial sectors, deregulation and privatisation.

The implementation of 'phase two' of this regeneration programme was postponed until after the 1978 parliamentary elections, but 'phase one', the counter-inflationary squeeze, was pursued with relish in 1976 and 1977. On 22 September 1976, within a month of assuming office, the new Prime Minister introduced the savage 'Barre Plan', comprising a three-month price freeze, a reduction in VAT, increases in income tax and car tax, higher interest rates and a curb on the growth of the money supply through the setting of new targets. These measures were geared towards reducing inflation from an annual rate of 11% to one of 6.5% within a year, even at the cost of higher unemployment. The scheme was determinedly implemented in 1977 and 1978 and was combined with tough and populist curbs on immigration.[1] Only minor deviations from this harsh new line were countenanced despite the imminence of elections.

The March 1978 National Assembly Elections

In May 1974 the Left Coalition, after coming within 400 000 votes of capturing the presidency, became convinced that it could finally achieve a National Assembly majority in the elections of March 1978 and plunge the French polity into a confused era of 'cohabitation'. This conviction was strengthened as unemployment mounted and recession deepened between 1974 and 1977. However, as the date of the Assembly elections approached, their outcome became less certain. Major changes had occurred within France's Right and Left coalitions, confusing the political landscape.

---

[1] Already, in 1974, a ban had been imposed on the immigration of non-EEC workers and the families of immigrant workers. In June 1977 the offer of a 10 000-francs repatriation bonus to unemployed immigrants was introduced.

Within the Right Coalition, the UDR had experienced a period of, first, introspective recrimination and then radical regeneration during the years between 1974 and 1978. Immediately after the May 1974 presidential election, traditional Gaullists, led by Michel Debré, blamed Chaban-Delmas' humiliating defeat on the back-stabbing of Jacques Chirac and his 'Gang of 43'. However, in the ensuing battle for party control it was Chirac who emerged victorious, being named party general-secretary by the UDR National Council in December 1974. Chirac then proceeded to work with his Pompidouiste allies Pierre Juillet and Marie-France Garaud and with Charles Pasqua to strengthen his control over the party machine. When he resigned as Prime Minister in August 1976, Chirac went a step further and radically refashioned the Gaullist party. He changed the name of the UDR to the *Rassemblement du Peuple pour la République (RPR)*, adopted a more right-wing, xenophobic and anti-communist programme and revived the use of mass rallies. This represented a return to the party's raw, populist roots and hierarchical form of organisation, with factory groups and branch federations being established in each of the country's 96 départements. Firmly at the head of this new party was Jacques Chirac, who was re-elected as a deputy for Corrèze and assumed floor leadership within the National Assembly.

This rightward shift in the RPR's policy stance encouraged the defection of many remnant 'Left Gaullists', but on balance the 'Chiracisation' of the RPR resulted in a rapid rise in membership from 285 000 in 1975 to over 700 000 in 1979. The party gained a further boost in March 1977 when its leader defeated Industry Minister Michel d'Ornano, President Giscard's preferred choice, in the inaugural race for the mayorship of Paris municipality. Chirac captured 60% of the second ballot vote and acquired in the process a significant new power base. This victory, which Chirac took as a sign of public support for his forceful, 'anti-left' campaigning approach, came as a severe blow to President Giscard and his attempts to construct a moderate new 'political centre'.

Giscard had used the years immediately following the May 1974 presidential election to reorganise and refashion his Independent Republican Party in preparation for a hoped-for major advance in 1978. His close ally, Michel Poniatowski, began this work in 1976, assuming day-to-day leadership of the party and bringing in groups of young new, liberal technocrats to work alongside the party's conservative old guard. Then, in 1977, the party was relaunched under the new name, the Republican Party (RP), and began to adopt a more avowedly centrist stance. It drew its ideological inspiration from President Giscard's new book *Démocratie Française* and began to develop close links with Jean Lecanuet's CDS. Two 'new wave' technocrats, Jean-Pierre Soisson and Jacques Blanc, were meanwhile brought in at the head of the party to revamp radically its organisation and broaden its activist base. This they were successful in doing, with membership of the IR/RP increasing rapidly from 100 000 in 1975 to 145 000 in 1979.

The 1978 parliamentary election thus occurred at a time when the two major parties within the Right Coalition diverged significantly in policy outlook, with each seeking dominance over the other in the new National Assembly. Despite this antagonism both sides recognised the imperative of agreeing to an electoral pact to present a united front against the Left Coalition. Talks on such a pact commenced in earnest during 1977 and operated on two levels. Jacques Chirac, leader of an RPR party whose popularity was climbing rapidly in the polls, was anxious to move the Right Coalition from its traditional employment of a seat-sharing pact towards a system of first ballot 'primaries' (see page 16), which he believed would favour the RPR. The other members of the Right Coalition, the RP, CDS and CNI, agreed, in July 1977, to such a shift to the primary system in three-quarters of the Assembly seats. To Chirac's surprise, however, these centre-right parties had at the same time been negotiating electoral pacts among themselves to present a common centre-right front in first ballot primaries, thus making RPR dominance less certain. In March 1978 this arrangement came out into the open when the loosely organised *Union pour la Démocratie Française (UDF)* was established, comprising the RP, CDS, CNI and Jean-Jacques Servan-Schreiber's unpredictable Radical Party. This institutionalised the division within the Right Coalition, leaving the electorate free to decide which faction was to emerge paramount after March 1978.

The Left Coalition similarly became bitterly divided during the years between 1974 and 1978 as a result of ideological differences and an intra-coalition competition for dominance. The Union of the Left, effected in 1972, had proved to be an electoral boon in 1973 and 1974, but the benefits had not been evenly divided between the PCF and PS. Georges Marchais, the PCF leader, had expected the Union, coupled with his intra-party 'democratisation' reforms, to broaden support for the Communists and enable them to break out of the ghetto of powerlessness. They would, he believed, retain their position as the leading party on the Left and be able to dominate the programme of any new Left Coalition government which achieved power. Unfortunately for the Communists, however, it was François Mitterrand's Socialist Party which emerged as the chief beneficiary of the Union, winning mounting support in the years between 1972 and 1977, establishing a powerful organisational base and drawing away working-class voters from the PCF.

This rise in support for the Socialist Party, which by January 1978 boasted a 7% poll lead over the PCF and presented itself as the single most popular party in France, was a serious threat to the Communists, who had always previously boasted paramountcy.[1] In addition, it threatened to change the power balance in any future Left Coalition government and encouraged the Socialists to be more assertive. This brought into the open the sharp intra-coalition ideological differences that had been papered over in the ambiguous 'Common Programme' of 1972. The Communist Party, despite its recent changes in policy outlook,[2] remained an unusually conservative and Stalinist body, which supported centralised and hierarchical government control, an anti-American and nationalistic approach to foreign affairs and a class-based, anti-capitalist, economic policy. The Socialist Party, by contrast, favoured a more internationalist approach to foreign affairs, political decentralisation at home, and reconciliation through 'workers' participation' at the workplace. Their approach to economic affairs also became progressively more moderate, accepting the possible need for short-term austerity sacrifices, as they attracted into the party a swathe of new centrist technocrats and as they sought to project themselves as a responsible and acceptable alternative government.

The conflict between the Communists and Socialists intensified between 1975 and 1977 with the PCF leadership bitterly denouncing Mitterrand and the PS for engaging in 'social democratic reformism'. These attacks proved, however, to be counterproductive, raising

---

[1] In January 1978 the PS national support rate stood at 28% compared with 21% each for the PCF and RPR and 16% for the RP. In 1972, by contrast, the PS-MRG and PCF stood neck-and-neck in the polls at 21%. Membership of the PS grew correspondingly from 70 000 in 1969 to 170 000 in 1978.

[2] The PCF's policy changes during these years were often bewildering and inconsistent. In February 1976, for example, it moved towards a 'Eurocommunist' line by dropping its historic commitment to the 'dictatorship' of the proletariat. A year later, it became a supporter of the French nuclear deterrent.

the popularity of the Socialist Party, which achieved significant advances in the cantonal elections of March 1976 and in the municipal elections of March 1977.[1] It was thus in a hostile atmosphere that the PCF, PS and Robert Fabre's MRG met in May 1977 to try to agree on an updated version of the 'Common Programme' for 1978. In these talks, the Communists were determined to have included in the new 'Common Programme' an increased number of their own policies, pressing in particular for a commitment to significantly increase the level of the minimum wage and to immediately nationalise 729 companies on assuming power. This proved too much for the MRG and Socialists. The MRG immediately walked out of the talks complaining of the drift towards 'statism or collectivism'. A week later the Socialists joined them, refusing to sanction the outright nationalisation of more than 277 companies. The five-year-old Union of the Left had thus been broken by a PCF which appeared to prefer electoral defeat to Socialist predominance and a divided opposition joined a divided majority in contesting the March 1978 Assembly elections.

The campaign for the election began as early as October 1977 for the RPR, with its leader Jacques Chirac energetically travelling over 30 000 miles to make almost 300 speeches. In these, he stressed the theme of 'freedom instead of collectivism' and warned the electorate of the dangers of voting for the 'socialo-communist' coalition. His campaign was climaxed by a huge RPR rally in Paris attended by 130 000 supporters. The UDF campaign began much later and lacked clear leadership, with President Giscard and Prime Minister Barre being able to give only indirect support. The Prime Minister did present, however, a UDF-influenced future programme for government, the 'Blois Programme', at Rambouillet on 6 January 1978 calling for 'reform, not upheaval; evolution not revolution' and repeatedly criticised the cost of the Left Opposition's reflationary economic programme during public debates. The President also periodically intervened with television messages to the electorate. As Head of State, he was unable to appear avowedly partisan. However, although stating his willingness to work with a Left Coalition government if returned, he warned of its dire possible economic and defence consequences

---

[1]   In March 1977 the Socialists won 83 and the PCF 72 of the mayorships in the 221 towns in France with a population in excess of 30 000 — a 50% gain for the Left Coalition.

and implored the electorate to act with 'responsibility' and to make the 'right choice' on voting day.

President Giscard's final public appeal on 11 March was particularly effective and helped to swing the result in the Right Coalition's favour. The Left Coalition, which had been damaged by continuing PCF-PS wrangling and by the PCF's refusal to enter into a Second Ballot withdrawal agreement until 13 March, gained 49.3% of the First Ballot vote on 12 March, its best ever post-war performance, compared to the Right Coalition's 46%. (The turnout at 83.3% was a record) When it came to the Second Ballot a week later, however, with 86% of seats still to be settled, public fears of political instability and a Communist voice in government resulted in a significant transfer of votes towards the government *majorité*. Almost a third of the voters who had supported the Socialist Party on the First Ballot, when faced with a Communist 'joint candidate' in their constituency, voted for a candidate from the Right Coalition, as voting discipline on the Left dissolved. The Right Coalition, which was divided more by personality than ideology, remained more cohesive. This enabled the government coalition, despite losing 14 seats, to retain a comfortable majority, gaining 291 of the 491 National Assembly seats (see Table 6), based on a 50.5%: 49.5% share of the Second Ballot vote. *Changement* (the victory of the Left) had been postponed.

TABLE 6 : THE MARCH 1978 NATIONAL ASSEMBLY ELECTION (1st Ballot)

	Votes	% of Total	Seats
UDF (Giscardians)	5.74m	20.4%	138
RPR (Gaullists)	6.30m	22.4%	153
Socialists & MRG	7.02m	25.0%	114
Communists	5.79m	20.6%	86
Far Right	0.91m	3.3%	—
Far Left	0.91m	3.3%	—
Other Left	0.81m	2.9%	—
Ecologists	0.61m	2.2%	—

However, although the March 1978 Assembly results did not lead to a dramatic change in executive power, significant changes did occur within each of the two Left and Right coalitions. In the Left Coalition, the Socialist Party captured more votes than the PCF for the first time since 1936 and established itself as the new dominant partner with the broadest geographical and social spread of support of any French party. Within the Right Coalition, the RPR, although still the largest single party, saw its share of the *majorité* vote fall from 70% in 1973 to only 49% in 1978, as it came under challenge from the new Giscardian UDF: the latter party now boasted almost half of the Right Coalition's Assembly seats.

Giscard's Swing Towards Conservatism: 1978-1981

The result of the March 1978 election, by increasing the size of the UDF bloc within the majority coalition, promised to strengthen the authority of President Giscard. In practice, however, although UDF deputies and technocrats dominated the new government, providing three-quarters of its members, President Giscard still remained dependent on RPR support for the passage of his policy programme. Such support proved, however, increasingly difficult to achieve during the second period of the Giscard presidency. The RPR leader, Jacques Chirac, remained in an embittered and vengeful mood, constantly criticising the President's policy initiatives. In 1979 and 1980, for example, he persuaded his RPR colleagues not to support the government's budget package, thus forcing Prime Minister Barre to invoke Article 49 and push through the measures by pledging the government's 'responsibility'. Chirac stopped short of bringing down the government on a confidence motion. His cavilling activities created uncertainty, however, in government minds and contributed to the increased caution and conservatism that became evident within the Giscard administration during its final three years in office.

Such conservatism was particularly evident in the social sphere, where, although Giscard did introduce minor packages targetted towards the handicapped and a non-compulsory scheme of workers' participation and share ownership, the reformist zeal of 1974/5 was no longer in evidence. Instead, many programmes were cut as a result of spending constraints. In the administrative and constitutional sphere, reformism was similarly abandoned as Giscard began to rule in an increasingly domineering and imperious manner, constantly interfering in all minor matters through his general staff team. The passage of the tough and controversial new 'Freedom and Security Law' in 1980, which, in response to mounting levels of violent crime and terrorism, significantly increased police powers and infringed upon civil rights, marked the apogee of Giscardian conservatism.

In foreign affairs, the Giscard administration proved to be more radical and enterprising, the President playing a leading role in the creation of the new European Monetary System (EMS) in 1979 and despatching French troops to Chad in an attempt to maintain stability following the outbreak of civil war. Similarly in its approach to the priority area of the economy, the Giscard-Barre team displayed a mixture of imagination and determination as they began to introduce 'phase two' of the Barre plan with the aim of effecting a major transformation in the climate within which French industrial firms operated.

This 'new liberal economic policy' sought to encourage French industries to be more efficient and internationally competitive through a process of disengaging the state from its paternalist regulatory activities. As a first, necessary step in this process, the huge and domineering Finance Ministry was broken down into two smaller, Economics and Budget, ministries in April 1978. This was followed by the announcement by Economics Minister René Monory that the statutory industrial price controls that had existed since 1948 would be lifted within six months for all goods excepting oil and pharmaceuticals. This radical reform formed the centrepiece of the new, more laissez-faire, economic strategy, and was aimed at enabling French industries to become both more independent in their forward planning and able to raise their domestic prices and thus accumulate profits for new plant modernisation investment. It was extended to the service and commercial sectors in 1979. The second key element in the new Giscard-Barre economic programme was a tightening in approach to the financing of nationalised industries. A sterner line was now taken to the bailing out of 'lame duck' industries: hopeless cases, for example the Marcel Boussac textile conglomerate and the Manufrance mail order group, being allowed to go to the wall. Secondly, reductions were made in the level of state subsidies in real terms, forcing public sector tariffs to be sharply raised in line with costs. Thirdly, small elements of 'privatisation' were sanctioned.

Taken together these deregulatory reforms represented a significant step away from traditional French *dirigisme* (state control) towards a more liberal, mixed economy approach. It should be stressed, however, that the Giscard-Barre team did not fully abandon dirigisme. The system of regional and national 'indicative planning' remained in place, while the central government selectively intervened to provide huge investment funds for three key industries vital to the nation's future: telecommunications, nuclear power and computers/high technology. State investment support was also provided to enable troubled industries which were seen to have a viable future to rationalise and modernise, while special aid and tax incentives were provided to depressed, strife-torn Lorraine to encourage the creation of new industries to replace its ailing steelworks.

President Giscard's prospects of re-election in 1981 depended, in large measure, upon the success of this new liberal economic strategy. In the short term, it had a stimulatory effect. France's GDP increased by 3.5% in 1978 and continued to grow during the first half of 1979, while inflation was held in check at 9.5%; the exchange rate stabilised and the trade balance returned to surplus. Unfortunately for the Giscard-Barre team, however, the new economic programme was disrupted by the twin shocks of the Iranian revolution (1978/9) and the outbreak of the Iran-Iraq war (September 1980) which led to a rapid quadrupling of world oil prices, plunging the world economy into a deep, new recessionary period. France, despite Giscard's ambitious nuclear power programme, remained heavily dependent upon Middle Eastern oil and was thus badly affected by the 1979-81 oil hike. Its consequences were the return of inflation to double digits and the trade balance into deficit and a sharp rise in unemployment from 1.3 million in 1978 to 1.68 million (7.3%) by early 1981.

Prime Minister Barre responded to the new economic crisis by tightening his deflationary fiscal stance. He continued to give priority to the fight against inflation at the expense of unemployment and called upon firms to modernise, rationalise and raise efficiency or perish. Barre's rigidly doctrinaire approach and the insensitivity he displayed towards the unemployed enraged the French public, rendering him, with only a 27% 'satisfaction rating', the most unpopular Prime Minister in recorded memory. This in turn lowered public support for President Giscard, who, having lost his early open vitality, had become an increasingly aloof and despondent figure subject to damaging gossip and court scandals.[1] As May 1981, the date for the next presidential election, approached, a *fin de siècle* atmosphere descended over the Élysée Palace. Giscard's re-election, which had appeared a formality as late as 1980, was now by no means certain.

---

[1] The most serious such scandal concerned Giscard's alleged acceptance of a gift of diamonds in 1973 from Emperor Jean-Bedel Bokassa, the deposed Central African Republic despot.

The May 1981 Presidential Election

Party Trends and Divisions: 1978-1981

Despite the unpopularity of the Barre austerity programme and the damage inflicted by government scandals, President Giscard's re-election in 1981 still appeared possible as a result of disorder and division in the ranks of his opponents.

In the Right Coalition, President Giscard could rely on the solid support of the UDF. This federation, with a combined membership of 300 000, was emerging as one of the most powerful and dynamic forces in French politics. At the local level it controlled a third of the nation's regional and département councils, while at the national level it topped the party poll in the June 1979 elections to the new European Parliament.[1] Elements within the UDF, most notably Jean-Jacques Servan-Schreiber's Radical Party which seceded in 1979, were concerned with the growing conservatism of Giscard's domestic policy approach. In general, however, the UDF was united behind the President's candidature.

This could not be said for the second party in the Right Coalition, Jacques Chirac's RPR. Chirac's combative and personalised style of leadership and his constant criticism of the Giscard administration's social, economic and foreign policies was bitterly opposed by moderate Gaullists led by Jacques Chaban-Delmas, Olivier Guichard and Justice Minister Alain Peyrefitte. More conservative old-guard Gaullists, including Michel Debré, approved of Chirac's nationalistic attacks on President Giscard and his calls for state intervention and reflation to deal with the scourge of unemployment, but disliked the manner in which the Gaullist movement had been transformed into a modern, structured party machine staffed by young, middle-class Chiraquian technocrats. Such opposition gained in strength following the humiliating performance of the RPR in the March 1979 cantonal elections and June 1979 Euro-elections, when it finished fourth behind even the

[1]   The UDF fought the June 1979 Euro-election under the banner the Union for France in Europe (UFE) and was led by the popular Health Minister Simone Veil. It captured 27.6% of the total vote, entitling it, under the party list PR system employed in this contest, to 25 seats, being followed by the Socialists (23.6%: 22 seats), the PCF (20.6%: 19 seats) and the RPR (16.3%: 15 seats). Both the UFE and PS fought on pro-European tickets, the PCF and RPR anti-European. However, with the turnout being only 60.7%, with many anti-EEC Gaullists abstaining, the poll was not fully reflective of public opinion.

PCF. Chirac attempted to respond to this criticism and adopted a more restrained tone from the spring of 1980. The damage had, however, been done and he was to find himself facing two intra-party challengers for the presidency in 1981: Michel Debré (69) and Marie-France Garaud (47).

The Left Opposition was equally divided, with the 1972-77 Union of the Left now in tatters. The PCF, which had moderated its stance and flirted with Eurocommunism in 1976, moved back towards a staunchly pro-Soviet line, refusing to condemn the Soviet invasion of Afghanistan in December 1979 or to support the Polish 'Solidarity' free trade union movement during 1980 and 1981. In addition, the party clamped down upon grass-roots calls for greater democratis-ation in its decision-making process at its 23rd Congress in May 1979. This abrupt *volte-face* created dissent within PCF ranks, with younger intellectuals, led by Louis Althusser and Jean Elleinstein, favouring a continuance of the 1970-77 democratisation, modern-isation, united-left strategy. The party polled a respectable 20.6% in the June 1979 Euro-elections, but was less confident about the prospects of its candidate, Georges Marchais, in 1981.

The other elements in the Left Alliance, the MRG radicals and the Socialist Party, were disheartened by their failure to grasp power in 1978. The MRG leader, Robert Fabre, rapidly left the Union and accepted the chairmanship of a commission to investigate unemployment for President Giscard in April 1978: a month later Michel Crepeau succeeded Fabre as MRG president. The Socialist Party, by contrast, while being pleased at having established itself as the dominant force on the Left and as the nation's most popular party — performing well in by-elections and cantonal polls between 1978-81 and controlling a third of provincial and metropolitan councils — was unsure as to how it would achieve a final break-through into power. The majority, led by François Mitterrand, favoured adhering to a solid left-wing policy programme and waiting for the Communists to rally to the Left banner on the Second Ballot of the 1981 presidential contest. They believed that the Socialists could still only achieve a majority with the support of both radical Centrist and Communist voters, but once elected would be in a position to dictate terms to these partners. Others within the party favoured, however, abandonment of the idea of formal or informal alliance with the PCF. They sought instead to establish the PS as a more moderate Social Democratic party, drawing in support from Centrists, ecologists and moderate Gaullists.

These differences in approach crystallised into a

personality-based battle for the party leadership and 1981 presidential nomination between Michel Rocard and François Mitterrand, with Pierre Mauroy standing in the wings as a possible compromise candidate. Rocard and Mauroy, 15 and 13 years the junior of Mitterrand respectively, represented a new younger generation of Socialists who a number within the party felt would outperform the twice unsuccessful Mitterrand, who would be 64 in 1981. Rocard, the son of a wealthy Protestant surgeon, was a brilliant *énarque* economist who had served in the Finance Inspectorate before entering politics in the mid-1960s. He first came to prominence as leader of the far-left PSU, contesting the 1969 presidential election, before joining the Socialists in 1975 and establishing a local base as mayor of Conflans (Paris). He was the leader of the flexible, anti-Communist Social Democratic wing of the party who opposed nationalisation and state planning, preferring instead a decentralised freer-market approach to the economy coupled with workers' control and environmentalism. Pierre Mauroy was, by contrast, a solid machine politician who, having trained as a teacher and worked for the FEN union, joined the PS and had slowly worked his way up from the rank of Socialist Youth Chief to the posts of mayor of Lille (1973-), chairman of the giant PS Northern Federation (1971-79) and party deputy leader. He was an orthodox *Mitterrandiste* in outlook.

Rocard took the lead in the intra-party battle for the presidential nomination between 1978-81, proving to be a most effective and engaging campaign speaker. He lacked, however, sufficient support within the Socialist Party to mount a successful challenge and soon found himself being outflanked by the wily Mitterrand, who allied himself with Jean-Pierre Chevènement's Marxist CERES grouping to defeat Rocard's Social Democratic programme at the April 1979 Metz Party Congress. A year later Mitterrand announced his intention to contest the 1981 presidential election 'in the interests of Socialist unity'. His nomination was ratified at the Special Party Congress in Creteil in January 1981, Rocard withdrawing his candidature.

The Candidates and the Campaign: January — May 1981

The quadripartite nature of modern French politics was most clearly demonstrated in the campaign for the presidency in May 1981. Ten candidates (seven men and three women) contested the First

Ballot, four being drawn from minority 'fringe parties' and two, Debré and Garaud, being rebels from within a major party.[1] The real battle centred, however, around four candidates drawn from each of the major parties: Jacques Chirac (48), representing the RPR; Georges Marchais (60), the PCF; François Mitterrand (64), the PS; and the incumbent Valéry Giscard d'Estaing (55), representing the UDF.

Chirac and Marchais both contested the election out of a sense of party obligation with only an outside prospect of achieving the first or second place which would entitle them to participate in the run-off Second Ballot. Chirac boasted strong support among farmers, shopkeepers, small businessmen and churchgoing Roman Catholics and from the west-central France and Paris metropolis regions, while Marchais could rely on bedrock communist support from the industrial north-east, the Midi and the Paris suburbs. Both looked forward to the opportunity of putting across their party message and sought a respectable 20% share of the vote, which might prove sufficient for a run-off position if the contest became tight. They were both supported by well-financed and well-organised party machines and proved to be the most energetic and controversial campaigners in 1981, drawing large audiences for both their public and television appearances.

Chirac, pledging large increases in the defence budget and adopting a strongly nationalistic and anti-Soviet policy line, presented himself as the most conservative of the leading candidates. He also continued to criticise President Giscard's economic strategy, proposing his own high-growth package of administrative economies and tax cuts. In this proposed programme Chirac combined elements of traditional Gaullism, including the call for greater workers' participation in industry, with a new Reaganite free-enterprise, deregulatory approach, as his thinking on economic matters evolved with the changing intellectual circumstances of the early 1980s.

Georges Marchais, the coarse, plebeian former metalworker, proved to be equally robust in a campaign which was directed

---

[1] There had been 64 prospective presidential candidates in 1980/1 but only 10 managed to gain the necessary backing from 500 elected officials from 30 *départements*. Those failing to gain sufficient signatures included the 'Left Gaullist' Michel Jobert (then leader of the Movement of Democrats), the National Front leader Jean-Marie Le Pen, the rebel Communist Roger Garaudy, the Trotskyist Alain Krivine and the popular clown Coluche, who had stood as an anti-politics candidate.

towards France's agitated blue-collar workers. He adopted a chauvinistic, moralistic and populist stance, campaigning against immigrant workers, drugs and the European Community, and proposing swingeing wealth and profit taxes to provide funds to create three million new jobs within four years. He pressed, in addition, for sweeping nationalisation, large-scale reflation, the limitation of defence spending to 3% of GNP and the immediate switch to a 35-hour working week.

Despite these energetic campaigns, when polling day arrived for the First Ballot on Sunday, 26 April, both Chirac and Marchais were eliminated, as expected, finishing in third and fourth positions respectively. (See Table 7.) Marchais' performance, the PCF's worst since 1936, was particularly disappointing and was further evidence of the continuing defection of communist voters towards the socialist camp. Chirac's showing was more heartening. He succeeded in raising his share of the poll from 10% to 18% during three months of campaigning and performed far more convincingly than Chaban-Delmas in 1974. In addition, Chirac outpolled his Gaullist rivals Debré and Garaud by a combined figure of 6:1. This exhibited his dominance within the RPR and left him in a position to establish himself as the future leader of the Right Coalition if Giscard failed in the Second Ballot on 10 May.

The contest for the Second Ballot became, as expected, a clear Right-Left battle between President Giscard and the 'great survivor' François Mitterrand. What was surprising, however, was the closeness of their performances in the First Ballot, with the incumbent President leading Mitterrand by a mere 2.5% and the

TABLE 7 : THE 1981 PRESIDENTIAL ELECTION FIRST BALLOT (Turnout 81%)

		Votes	%
Giscard	(UDF)	8.22m	28.3%
Mitterrand	(PS)	7.50m	25.8%
Chirac	(RPR)	5.22m	18.0%
Marchais	(PCF)	4.46m	15.3%
Lalonde	(Ecologist)	1.13m	3.9%
Mlle Laguiller	(Far Left)	0.67m	2.3%
Crepeau	(MRG)	0.64m	2.2%
Debré	(RPR)	0.48m	1.7%
Mme Garaud	(RPR)	0.39m	1.3%
Mme Bouchardeau	(PSU)	0.32m	1.1%

broad Right and Left groupings running neck-and-neck when the results of all candidates were combined. The narrowing of the gap between these two contestants became increasingly evident in opinion polls from November 1980 onwards and was the result of a combination of factors: the poor campaigning tactics of the Giscard team; growing public antipathy to the President's style of government and economic record; and the emergence of François Mitterrand as an attractive and credible alternative presidential figure.

President Giscard began his 1981 presidential campaign in an overly confident mood. He ran as an above-party 'citizen candidate' in an aloof manner, arguing that his first term had been one of success, combining modernising social reform with a sensible new economic policy and a firm, but flexible, approach to foreign affairs. He offered a similar recipe of safe, moderate 'reform within the established order' for his second term, with the addition of an immigrant repatriation and early retirement package which, it was hoped, would reduce unemployment by one million within four years. The style and tone of Giscard's campaign proved, however, to be largely negative and failed to inspire or convince French electors. It was run by the powerful, former ministerial, troika of Jean-François Deniau, Jean-Philippe Lecat and Monique Pelletier, but lacked the benefit of UDF activist support as a result of the President's determinedly non-partisan stance. The campaign became largely reactive with the President finding himself being attacked from all sides, Right, Left and Centre, during the run-up to the First Ballot. This lacklustre performance, coupled with growing public antipathy to President Giscard as a result of government scandals and the worsening economic climate, provided fertile ground for a successful challenge form the Left and the opportunity was eagerly grasped by François Mitterrand.

François Mitterrand was depicted by the Giscard team as a 'man of the past' and an inveterate loser who was making a final tilt at the presidency simply because the Socialist Party could not decide upon and unite around a new successor. They were wrong, however, to belittle their opponent who had proved himself during the years since 1947 to be one of the nation's wiliest and most resilient political tacticians and who was to project himself as a reassuring presidential figure in 1981.

The reserved and reflective Mitterrand was a complex and enigmatic character. Born into a middle-class Catholic station-master's family in the small town of Jarnac near Cognac in south-

57

western France in October 1916, he had attended university in Paris during the mid 1930s where he read law and politics and immersed himself in French literature. During this period he developed a sympathy for the democratic traditions of Republican France, an aversion to bourgeois-aristocratic privilege and a humanistic belief in liberty and justice. He first made his mark during the Second World War when, after being seriously wounded and taken prisoner by the German army, he escaped to Vichy France in December 1941 and became an energetic Resistance leader, organising the repatriation of PoWs and deportees and being awarded, like Giscard, the Croix de Guerre.

After the war, Mitterrand concentrated upon a political career and gained election to the National Assembly for the rural Nièvre constituency north-west of Dijon in 1946. His political philosophy remained vague, although he stood on an anti-communist ticket and aligned himself with the small centre-left 'Democratic and Socialist Union of the Resistance' (DSUR) grouping. Mitterrand, as a result of his wartime record, proceeded to gain ministerial posts in eleven of the Centrist governments during the years between 1947 and 1958, serving successively as minister for war veterans, information, overseas territories, interior and justice. It was, however, de Gaulle's assumption of power in the putsch of June 1958 which marked the turning-point in Mitterrand's political career, radicalising and transforming him into a committed leader of the Left.

Mitterrand despised de Gaulle, viewing him as a representative of France's old and failed right-wing officer corps élite. He also disliked his authoritarian streak and thus became one of the few Fourth Republic political figures, outside of the PCF, to vote against de Gaulle's investiture and the creation of the Fifth Republic. As a consequence of this, Mitterrand lost his Assembly seat in the landslide election of November 1958. He rapidly bounced back, however, with a new determination, strengthening his local base in the Nièvre area, where he was elected mayor of Château Chinon and Senate representative. During these years, Mitterrand also constructed a new anti-Gaullist centre-left *Union of Democratic Forces* composed of former DSUR politicians, SFIO rebels (a forerunner group to the PSU) and Pierre Mendès-France's Radical Party left-wingers and built up the new *Convention of Republican Institutions (CRI)*, merging together the DSUR with more than 50 Republican Political Clubs.

Mitterrand decided to leave the Catholic church during the early

1960s and became more radical in outlook. He regained election to the National Assembly in 1962 and three years later made his mark on the national stage as the Left's last-minute representative in the presidential race against de Gaulle. He replaced Gaston Defferre, the moderate SFIO mayor of Marseilles, whose campaign failed to take off, and rapidly set up the new broad-based Federation of the Left, comprising the SFIO, Radical Party and CRI, to support his candidature. Mitterrand cultivated a youthful, forward-looking, anti-establishment image and, gaining the tacit support of the PCF, who did not put up a separate candidate of their own, performed well, capturing 45% of the Second Ballot vote.

This Federation remained in force and was improved after 1965, an opposition 'shadow cabinet', for example, being established. Mitterrand also pressed for closer electoral links with the PCF, successfully achieving a Second Ballot pact agreement for the 1967 Assembly elections. The May 1968 'events', during which Mitterrand precipitately called for de Gaulle's resignation and the establishment of a replacement Left government, temporarily set back this unification strategy. In 1971/2, however, Left unity was finally achieved, based around the new Socialist Party, which Mitterrand joined and led, and the left-wing 'Common Programme' agreement with the PCF. It enabled Mitterrand to come within a whisker of capturing the presidency in 1974 and, although the PCF had by 1981 officially seceded from the Left Alliance, the Socialist leader upheld its principles in the new knife-edged contest.

Mitterrand fought in 1981 on his own personal manifesto, '110 Propositions for France', which incorporated elements of the 1972 'Common Programme' and the Socialist Party's 1980 'Plan for France in the Eighties'. This programme included the traditional calls for nationalisation, decentralisation and liberalisation and included a specific 'economic emergency plan' designed to eradicate unemployment through a combination of increased state investment, additional hiring by the public sector (with the aim of employing 210000 extra people by 1982) and a shortening of the working week to 35 hours by 1985. Mitterrand pledged, in addition, to reduce social inequality through raising the minimum wage and imposing a new wealth tax and promised to introduce a constitutional reform to shorten or restrict the presidential term. This clear and simple document provided a check-list for prospective voters in an attractive 'catch-all' manner.

Mitterrand's campaign was run by the experienced party figures of Mauroy, Defferre, Rocard and Chevènement, and drew upon the marketing advice of Jacques Segula to improve presentation. Mitterrand's handlers decided to make use of their candidate's age, experience and assured demeanour, building up the image of *La Force Tranquille*, presenting Mitterrand as a calm, courageous, patriotic and mystical man of destiny who exuded a quiet inner strength and who promised 'reform without revolution'. In public meetings, Mitterrand retained his strength as a witty and lyrical orator. On television, however, he adopted a solemn, statesmanlike manner, projecting himself as a figure seeking to unite the nation and to bring the forces of the Left back into government circles. Combined with this 'presidentialist strategy' were constant criticisms of Giscard, who was depicted as an autocrat who had divided the nation and presided over 'failure on all fronts'.

This twin-pronged campaign strategy proved to be remarkably effective, enabling Mitterrand to gain a comfortable second place in the First Ballot. As the campaigning for the Second Ballot moved underway it became clear that Mitterrand was better placed than in 1974 and might finally defeat Giscard on 10 May. Firstly, Giscard d'Estaing's youthful and liberal image of 1974 had been tarnished by seven years in office and his reputation for economic expertise had been dented by the severe 1979-81 recession. Secondly, the Giscardian centre-right coalition which had been constructed in 1974 was in disarray. A number of Centrist figures, including Jean-Jacques Servan-Schreiber's Radical Party, deserted the President as a result of his economic and social strategy, while many RPR politicians withheld their support. Jacques Chirac declared on 27 April, after the First Ballot, that he would personally vote for Giscard, but advised his supporters themselves to vote according to conscience. Michel Debré gave Giscard only qualified backing while Marie-France Garaud stated that she would cast a blank vote. Component social and interest groups within the Giscardian coalition also deserted the President in 1981 as a result of distaste for his 1974-81 policy programme. For example, a large proportion of the 650 000-strong French Jewish community switched away from Giscard in opposition to his alleged pro-Arab foreign policy, while many farmers deserted as a result of the fall in farm incomes between 1974-81.

By contrast, the Left Coalition proved to be more cohesive during 1981. Georges Marchais, the PCF leader, criticised Mitterrand during the first round, depicting him as a moderate rightist, but called on PCF voters to support him in the Second Ballot. This call

TABLE 8 : THE MAY 1981 PRESIDENTIAL ELECTION (Second Ballot)

VOTING BY SOCIAL GROUPS

	Giscard	Mitterrand
Farmers	68%	32%
Retired	55%	45%
Small Shopkeepers/ Self-Employed	64%	36%
Top Managers & Professionals	55%	45%
Lower Managers/ White-Collar Workers	38%	62%
Ordinary Workers	28%	72%

Fig. 3

Mitterrand's share of the vote
More than 60%   50 - 55%
55 - 60%   Less than 50%

was echoed by the defeated MRG, PSU and Trotskyist candidates. The base of the 'Mitterrand coalition' was also, most significantly, expanding. The lowering of the voting age to 18 brought in a swathe of young new voters, a category which had traditionally supported the Left, while many female voters turned away from Giscard disappointed by his halting feminist reforms. Mitterrand also drew into his coalition many of the 1.1 million environmentalists who had supported Brice Lalonde on the First Ballot and who were attracted by the Socialists' promise of a referendum on nuclear power. Most important of all, however, was the enticement of many crucial Centrist voters into the Mitterrand camp. They sought greater economic and social change and now felt safe voting for Mitterrand, believing the danger of Communist dominance in a Left government to be much reduced.

When voting day arrived on 10 May the swing towards Mitterrand was confirmed. The electoral turnout rose to 85.9% and François Mitterrand swept to a narrow, but convincing, victory by 15.7 million votes (51.8% of the total) to 14.6 million (48.2%). The candidate of the Left polled most strongly in the traditional Socialist strongholds of north-eastern, southern and south-western France, but also made significant progress in the Catholic and conservative west and recorded a majority in 65 of the nation's 96 metropolitan départements. (See Figure 3.) His victory also rested heavily upon the support of middle and lower socioeconomic groups and the young. (See Table 8.) What proved decisive, however, for Mitterrand was the 90% backing he received from Communist voters, the 2:1 transfer of ecologist voters to his candidature and the failure of Chirac supporters to move solidly behind Giscard on the Second Ballot: only 71% turning to Giscard.

The two key reasons for Giscard's defeat were the public's growing antipathy to his style of presidency and their concern at the mounting level of unemployment. The latter consistently topped opinion polls as the key campaign issue. A third, important factor was the popular desire for change and reform to bring the French institutional structure in line with contemporary society, completing the work left unfinished in 1976. François Mitterrand and the Socialist Party most accurately reflected the mood and aspirations of this secular, urban, white-collar 'New France' and were at last given the opportunity of managing the nation's affairs after 23 years of rule by the Right.

The National Assembly Elections of June 1981

Although François Mitterrand was granted a presidential mandate on 10 May, he lacked a majority in the National Assembly to push through his proposed programmes. It thus appeared that the country was set for a period of constitutional crisis and a trial of strength between the President and Prime Minister which would finally put to the test the vague Debré-de Gaulle constitution of 1958. Such a crisis was surprisingly averted, however, by the French electorate when called to vote in new National Assembly elections on 28 June.

François Mitterrand stated in advance his determination to immediately dissolve the National Assembly and call fresh elections if elected to the presidency. This pledge was duly carried out on 21 May, with an interim Left Coalition government being appointed in the meantime headed by Pierre Mauroy to take charge of the nation's inter-election affairs. The prospects of the Left gaining a majority in the parliamentary election appeared promising following the advances of 1973 and 1978. It seemed likely, however, that the Socialist Party would lack a majority on its own and would be dependent upon Communist support, thus allowing the PCF to dictate terms to the new administration. This vexed domestic and foreign political observers. In reality, however, things did not work out this way. As the campaign for the June elections progressed, it rapidly became clear that the Socialists would perform far better than expected and the prospect of a single-party majority began to emerge. Two factors explained this dramatic turn of events: the dejected and confused state of the Right Coalition and the continued rallying of Centrist and Communist supporters towards the presidential banner.

The UDF was left rudderless and disorientated by the events of 10 May. Its leader Giscard sullenly took a political sabbatical, leaving his colleagues, fearing electoral annihilation, to negotiate a First Ballot joint-candidate agreement with the RPR. In this pact, which sought to secure the future of incumbent deputies and minimise First Ballot eliminations, only one, jointly-agreed, Right Coalition candidate contested each seat under the banner 'Union for a New Majority' (UNM). The price of such an agreement was, however, high for the UDF, as effective leadership of the Right Coalition was now handed over to their *bête noire*, Jacques Chirac, a man accused by Raymond Barre of having played 'double or quits with the fate of the Fifth Republic' in May.

This 'United Front' strategy failed, however, to prevent a Socialist landslide victory in the Second Ballot on 21 June as the public rallied to the presidential banner. Early signs of a surge of support for Mitterrand and the Socialists became clear as early as 10 May when the presidential election predictions were announced. A crowd of more than 150 000 gathered in Paris and marched towards the Place de la Bastille, the nation's republican gathering-point, and raised red standards to celebrate the *changement*. Similar spontaneous demonstrations broke out in provincial cities all across the country. The new Mitterrand-Mauroy government built upon this wave of euphoric optimism by rapidly passing a series of populist reforms, raising welfare benefits by more than 20% and the minimum wage by 10%, thus making clear their determination to help the poor and to reduce income inequalities if given the means in the June elections. Such actions were geared towards attracting working-class, former Communist, voters into the Socialist camp. More moderate and middle-class Centrist voters were wooed by intimations by Mitterrand and Mauroy that a future Socialist government would be realistic and restrained and would not yield to PCF ultimatums.

This dual-pronged approach, appealing to both the Left and Centre, the working and middle-classes, proved to be remarkably successful when votes were cast for the First Ballot on 14 June. The Socialists succeeded in prising away around a third of the Communist vote and a sixth of the Right Coalition's 1978 support. They thus vaulted from the 25% mark to garner an astonishing 38% of the national vote on the crucial First Ballot: the best single party

TABLE 9 : THE JUNE 1981 NATIONAL ASSEMBLY ELECTION

	(1st Ballot)		(Metropolitan)
	Votes	% of Total	Seats
Socialists & MRG	9.38m	37.8%	286
RPR (Gaullists)	5.19m	20.9%	83
UDF (Giscardians)	4.77m	19.2%	61
Communists	4.00m	16.1%	44
Far Left	0.33m	1.3%	—
Far Right	0.75m	3.0%	—
Other Left	0.14m	0.6%	—
Ecologists	0.27m	1.1%	—

performance recorded during the Fifth Republic. (See Tables 4 and 9: the turnout, at 71%, was, however, unusually low, with many Right Coalition voters abstaining). This left the Socialists and their MRG allies in a position to sweep the board when the third-placed Communist candidates stood aside for the Second Ballot on 21 June. They more than doubled their parliamentary representation and captured 289 seats in the new, 491-member, Assembly.

The result of the June 1981 elections highlighted the peculiarities of the Fifth Republic electoral system in the new era of coalition pacts. It also displayed the allure of the presidency and was a graphic example of the 'coat-tails' effect, as the French public provided their new President with the parliamentary tools to fulfil his mandate free of dependency on the PCF, thus ensuring political stability. The election was a major blow to the parties of the Right and an ominous one for the PCF. The Right Coalition was decimated, losing half its deputies, including the influential figures of Peyrefitte, Deniau, Lecat, Roger Chinaud and Yves Guena, and experienced humiliating defeat in strongholds such as Brittany, Lorraine, Corsica and the Auvergne. Inside the National Assembly it was forced to surrender control of commission chairs and was consigned to the position of opposition in the weak French parliamentary system. However, although such a level of defeat came as a jarring shock to the Right Coalition, it could commence work on reconstruction and could hope to win back power in 1986 if the Mitterrand team failed to turn around the French economy. Matters were more serious for the PCF. It had been trounced convincingly by the Socialist Party in the second election running, had lost a large slice of its support, particularly in the Paris region, and was now firmly the second party of the Left, lacking real bargaining power. The party appeared threatened with irreversible decline and seemed destined to become a mere appendage in the French political system unless some means was found of reviving its fortunes.

The Giscard Presidency: A Retrospective Assessment

The twin defeats of May and June 1981 consigned Giscard d'Estaing and the Right Coalition to the political wilderness for a quinquennium and stimulated a prolonged period of introspective inquiry. In retrospect, however, the record of the Giscard administration was not as barren as had appeared to French electors in May 1981.

In foreign affairs, the President had displayed imagination and had taken a lead in transforming the European Community into a more co-operative, cohesive and forward-looking force, instituting the system of informal, quarterly heads of government meetings (the European Council) and playing a prominent role in the creation of the European Parliament and EMS. Giscard also made efforts to improve relations with the United States and involve France more directly in NATO military structures.

At home, the economic record of the Giscard administration was, by comparative standards, most creditable. During a difficult period for the world economy, France recorded the highest average growth rate, 2.8% per annum, of any industrialised country with the exception of Japan during the years between 1974 and 1981. In addition, its record on inflation and unemployment (although the latter's level more than tripled between 1974 and 1981) was bettered only by the United States, Japan and Germany, and it bequeathed to its successors a well-controlled budget, currency and balance of payments. The Giscard team could also boast that, through their 'new liberal economic policy', they had freed French industry of many overweening state controls and encouraged firms to modernise and rationalise in a more efficient manner. Furthermore, they had given specific encouragement to new high-tech and telecommunications industries and had reduced French dependency on outside energy sources from 70% in 1974 to only 50% in 1981 as a direct result of their new nuclear energy programme.

It was rather in the social and administrative spheres that the record of the Giscard presidency was more disappointing and chequered. The early liberal and pluralistic reforms of 1974-76 gave way to domineering conservatism after 1976, partly as a result of pressure from within the Right Coalition and partly as a result of Giscard's own loss of reformist zeal. Giscard thus bequeathed to his successor an overly centralised state, a powerful, officious and intrusive presidential system, an outmoded legal system and a society still riven by a wide chasm between rich and poor. It was his successor's administration which set out to rectify these imbalances, as the pendulum swung towards the Coalition of the Left.

The Mitterrand Presidency: 1981 —

The Mitterrand Style and Method of Governing

François Mitterrand made his reputation during the early years of the Fifth Republic as the implacable opponent of the concept of a strong presidency. However, although he continued to criticise the excessive concentration of power in presidential hands during the 1981 election campaign, once installed he proved loth, as Presidents before him, to relinquish the accumulated powers of office. The Mitterrand period thus witnessed subtle changes in style rather than a substantive reordering of the French executive power structure.

The first and most basic change effected under the Mitterrand presidency was that of personnel. Of particular importance was the shake-up effected within the nation's administrative élite, as the Giscardian State was gradually dismantled and replaced with a new, Socialist-minded, Mitterrandiste state. This was achieved through a gradual purge of obstructive senior civil servants, police chiefs, intelligence service directors, university rectors, nationalised industry bosses, television network heads and two-thirds of the nation's prefects, and their replacement with new officials sympathetic to the Socialist strategy. Secondly, changes were effected in the composition of the Economic and Social Council and, as a result of the June elections, in leadership of the nation's Regional Councils, 13 of the 22 now becoming Socialist controlled. Finally, within the Élysée Palace there was an even more extensive turnover of personnel as a new 'general staff' team was put together under the direction of the chief of staff Pierre Bérégovoy (55). This team was more varied in character than that of its predecessor, including in its ranks not only former civil servant technocrats and personal friends of the President, but also a swathe of former Socialist Party workers, professionals, academics and even the odd former factory worker. Its key figures were Jacques Fournier (51), deputy chief of staff, André Rousselet (59), head of the President's private 'cabinet', and Jacques Attali (38), the former *énarque* economist who was to emerge as the President's free-ranging ideas man.

When it came to methods of running this government machine, significant changes in style soon became more evident during the Mitterrand presidency. The new President stepped easily into his new office and developed a grand, almost pontifical, manner during his addresses to the French public, recalling in many respects the early de Gaulle. Despite this lofty demeanour, however, Mitterrand's government operated in a more relaxed and informal manner than that of any of his predecessors. There was greater discussion of options and alternatives within the Élysée Palace, Council of Ministers (with its 'inner cabinet' of six) and *Conseils restreints*; ministers were given a greater latitude to make policy decisions in non-key areas; and the 'general staff' team, although its influence increased perceptibly over the years, was restrained from interfering incessantly in the day-to-day affairs of individual ministries. The President still remained the chief policy-maker in the political executive and the Élysée staff most influential. However, the style of governing became more co-operative during the Mitterrand years.

The new Socialist government enjoyed the major advantage over its predecessor of holding its own large majority within the National Assembly. This freed it from the dependency upon the whims of a fickle coalition partner which had proved so debilitating for the Giscard administration. The Mitterrand government did, however, face a number of important policy-making constraints. The most obvious were those of the Senate, in which there was a 2:1 centre-right majority over the parties of the Left, Conseil d'État and Constitutional Council. Of even greater importance, however, were the internal factional divisions within the Socialist Party and government itself. 50% of the Socialist Deputies elected to parliament in June 1981 were mainstream Mitterrandistes, 20% were supporters of Rocard, 15% supported the pragmatic Mauroy and 12% aligned themselves with the 'hard left' CERES grouping. These factions differed over the amount and pace of change desired: the Rocard 'social democrat', technocrat grouping favouring a cautious and realistic 'minimalist' approach, the CERES faction pressing for immediate radical, 'maximalist' reform and the Mitterrand and Mauroy groups preferring a steady, but firm, intermediate approach. Great skill was thus required in keeping the diverse elements within the party united and contented.

President Mitterrand did not, however, just face the problem of party factionalism. Having made his reputation as the leader of a broad Union of the Left and having been dependent upon the votes of supporters of Centrist and Communist parties in the Second Ballot of the presidential election of 1981, the new President chose to go outside the confines of his own party and construct a government composed of 'all the (radical) forces' in France. He sought to be seen as a unifying, above-party, ruler and thus brought into his new government of June 1981 leading figures from the radical centrist MRG (Michel Crepeau — Environment; François Abadie — Tourism), the former Gaullist foreign minister and current leader of the Movement of Democrats, Michel Jobert (Foreign Trade), and four members of the PCF (deputy leader Charles Fiterman — Transport; Anicet Le Pors — Civil Service; Jack Ralite — Health; and Marcel Rigout — Professional Training).

President Mitterrand's granting of four, albeit minor, ministries to Communists, the first time this had happened since 1947, was controversial, earning an immediate rebuke from the new American Vice-President George Bush. It was, however, effected on Mitterrand's own terms and proved to be of both short- and long-term tactical value. The new President, recalling how, during his student days, Léon Blum's Popular Front government of 1936/7 had, after failing to include Communists in its ranks, been brought down within 13 months by a wave of CGT inspired strikes, was understandably anxious to protect his flanks. He thus forced the PCF leadership to sign, on 23 June, a 'Joint Government Pact' whereby the PCF committed itself to 'flawless solidarity' within the government and at the local and factory level, agreed to support the government's two-year economic recovery programme and recognised that reform would occur at a cautious pace in the difficult circumstances of the early 1980s. This agreement effectively ensured the new government two years of goodwill and industrial peace from the CGT. The PCF was, next, forced to make a number of humiliating concessions in domestic and foreign policy areas: agreeing to lower its sights on nationalisation and to back calls for the withdrawal of Soviet troops from Afghanistan and support for the Polish 'Solidarity' free trade union. Such agreements were of long-term benefit to President Mitterrand, who sought to end the 'Communist Problem' in France by either fully integrating them into the French polity as a more liberal and democratic entity or fully destroying them through eroding their identity and political base.

The inclusion of Communist ministers did carry the risk for President Mitterrand of exacerbating the radical-moderate factional divisions which existed within the new cabinet. Fortunately for the President, however, the four Communist 'guests' proved to be loyal and model ministers who worked well with cabinet and senior civil service colleagues. Thus during the years that followed, the arch bargainer and manipulator François Mitterrand was able successfully to weld his diverse ministerial team together into a largely united whole and concentrate upon achieving a Socialist transformation of the French polity and society.

The Policy Aims of the Mitterrand Administration

François Mitterrand ascended to the presidency at the age of 64 determined to make a lasting impression on French history. He sought to carry out major and irreversible social and structural reforms, in the manner effected by the de Gaulle 'United Front' government of 1944-47 and the British Labour government of 1945-51, which would redress the balance in French society towards the 'People of the Left', the poor and underprivileged, and create a new 'French model of civilisation' and model of socialism which would be emulated elsewhere.

The Mitterrand administration sought, firstly, to effect a substantial redistribution of income from rich to poor in the notoriously inequitably balanced French society and to improve social and welfare facilities. It, secondly, called for major structural economic reform, with nationalisation and the extension of workers' rights and participation at its core. Such a programme would involve the state takeover of key modern industries and their infusion with substantial investment capital to transform them into model 'leading sectors' able to compete with the most modern Japanese *zaibatsus* (industrial combines). This new dynamic form of nationalisation would be coupled with a return to a more active form of state economic planning after the partial retreat of the Giscard years. The Mitterrand team sought, thirdly, to effect a thorough overhaul of the political and legal institutions of the Fifth

Republic, with the aim of creating a more open, liberal, pluralist, tolerant and democratic polity and society. Decentralisation was to be the key to such reform.

In addition to these ambitious long-term structural goals the new administration, assuming power at a time of severe economic crisis, was forced to give priority to the implementation of a shorter-term recovery programme to foster economic expansion and employment creation. This 'emergency programme' combined large-scale reflation, a growth in the budgetary deficit, a boost to public sector employment and special measures such as a lowering of the retirement age and a shortening of the working week. It was intended to work hand-in-hand with the administration's longer-term industrial regeneration programme. In practice, however, conflicts did emerge between the long- and short-term goals of the Mitterrand administration, with it becoming increasingly difficult to fund its ambitious social programme. This forced a radical shift in policy approach in the years after 1983.

The 'Socialist Experiment' in Practice: 1981-1983

The ministerial team of 44 members assembled by President Mitterrand in June 1981, although lacking recent experience of central administration, boasted 24 mayors and a clutch of former civil servants, party administrators and skilled academics. It thus possessed ample intellectual and administrative ability for the implementation of its policy programme.

In policy outlook, the cabinet was dominated by *Mitterrandistes* and Mauroyites. Michel Rocard was granted the senior post of Minister for Planning and Jean-Pierre Chevènement the important Research and Technology portfolio, with four of his CERES colleagues, Nicole Questiaux, Edwige Avice, Edmond Hervé and François Autain, also receiving ministerial posts. The bulk of the cabinet team was, however, drawn from the 'soft left' of the party, its key figures being: Jacques Delors (55), a former government economist and adviser to Chaban-Delmas, who became Minister for the Economy and Finance; Claude Cheysson (61), a former EEC Commission diplomat, who became Foreign Minister; Charles Hernu (57), a longstanding CRI Republican Club associate of the President, who became Defence Minister; Pierre Dreyfus, the former chairman of Renault, who became Industry Minister; and Robert Badinter and Gaston Defferre (70), who assumed the Justice and Interior portfolios.[1] At the head of the team was Pierre Mauroy (53), the cheerful, conciliatory and affable Socialist Party *apparatchik*, who became Prime Minister, contrasting sharply with his dour predecessor, Raymond Barre.

During the early months of the administration a mass of social and institutional reforms were rushed through the National Assembly by a ministerial team intoxicated with its newly acquired powers. These measures included the introduction of higher minimum wage, pension and family allowances and the imposition of higher wealth and luxury taxes noted above; the abolition of the death penalty and the State Security Court (a secret tribunal established by de Gaulle which had recently been used to try Breton and Corsican terrorists); the repeal of the 1980/1 'Security and Liberty' law; the improvement in the legal aid system; the abandonment of the scheme to introduce computerised identity cards; the licensing of 'free radio stations'; the improved treatment of immigrant workers; the reduction in the working week to 39 hours, with five weeks' paid holiday a year; and the introduction of voluntary retirement on a half pension at the age of 60. Taken together, these reforms represented a considerable advance in terms of justice, equality and liberty and brought France closer in line with its German, Anglo-Saxon and Scandinavian neighbours.

Many of these reforms were, however, 'easy' and obvious measures, taking up from where the Giscard team left off in 1976. The more central, far-reaching and imaginative reforms of the Mitterrand team were its decentralisation and nationalisation initiatives and its emergency economic recovery programme.

The Mitterrand administration's decentralisation reforms were termed, by Prime Minister Mauroy, the *'grande affaire du septennat'* and promised to be the most important institutional change effected in the French polity since 1962. To some extent they marked the culmination of more than a decade of reform which had included the formation of a new tier of indirectly elected Regional Councils in 1973 and President Giscard's creation of the Paris town council and regional councils for Corsica and the Île-de-France. In other respects, however, the decentralisation reforms of 1981/2 marked a radical and novel new departure and were a reflection of the thinking and philosophy of the previously excluded French

---

[1] The cabinet contained ten énarques (including Rocard, Fabius, Chevènement and Cheysson), nine academics, three men with ministerial experience during the Fourth Republic (Mitterrand, Defferre and Savary) and one during the Fifth Republic (Jobert).

Left. Politicians from the Right, including President Giscard, had favoured decentralisation in the economic sphere, creating the regional councils to act as advisers to the DATAR (*Délégation à l'Aménagement du Territoire et à l'Action Régionale*) planning agency and extending 'block grants' to local councils. They firmly opposed, however, any significant devolution of political power, which was seen as likely to endanger the unity of the 'One and Indivisible Republic'. Many within the Socialist Party were, by contrast, firm champions of political decentralisation. They viewed it as a means of infusing greater democratic participation and accountability into the overly centralised Fifth Republic. In addition, they saw such a devolution of power to be in the party's own interests, enjoying as it did such a firm base at the local, especially urban, government level.

Prime Minister Mauroy and Interior Minister Defferre, both prominent local political bosses, were particularly committed to decentralisation and gave priority to this issue upon assuming power in June 1981. A decentralised reform bill was thus quickly framed, debated in the National Assembly and approved in January 1982. Minor alterations were made following its scrutiny by the Constitutional Council and the bill was finally made law in March 1982. This major piece of legislation, the 'Defferre Law', radically altered the nature of French local government as a result of the three sets of changes it instituted. Firstly, it introduced direct elections to the nation's previously indirectly elected Regional Councils: the first such elections taking place in March 1986. Secondly, it downgraded the role of the prefect (now termed *Commissaire de la République*) at the département and regional level, replacing him as council chief executive by an elected member and depriving him of the powers of direct *a priori* supervision (*tutelle*). Thirdly, département and regional councils were given greater autonomy in policy making in their spheres of interest and were promised greater powers to raise finance locally, Prime Minister Mauroy stating that he envisaged local government's direct share of total tax revenue rising from the 1981 level of 18% towards one of 25-30%.

This reform fell well short of a federal devolution of power on the West German, Spanish or American models.[1] The centrally

---

[1] Greater power was devolved to Corsica, the centre of a violent, though minority-led, secessionist movement, which was granted its own directly elected parliament with the power to scrutinise National Assembly bills and to propose changes applicable to Corsica. The first elections to this assembly were held in August 1982.

appointed *commissaire* retained control over the local police machine, co-ordinated state services at the local level, exerted *a posteori* control over council budgets through the Court of Accounts and remained the vital connecting figure between localities and the central government and bureaucracy in Paris. Local councils were also still heavily dependent upon the centre for financial grants and for the technical and planning expertise which was provided by its administrative 'field services'. Despite these qualifications, however, the 'Defferre Law' represented a significant step away from Jacobin centralism and served to add weight to the concept of regionalism and enhance the power, prestige and importance of local and regional council members.

The nationalisation programme was equally of crucial importance to the Mitterrand administration, being viewed as a measure of political, social and economic significance. François Mitterrand had begun his political career as an opponent of nationalisation, but his views changed during the 1960s and 1970s, being influenced by the theoretical work of Jean-Pierre Chevènement. In his book *The Rose in the Fist* (1973), Mitterrand began to argue that growing concentration of ownership within industry and the emergence of multinationals had created private monopolies extracting 'super profits' from consumers and acting in a manner detrimental to the French national interest, choosing to invest, for example, in cheap labour sites abroad rather than at home. Mitterrand thus came to see nationalisation as a means of altering the power structure, of giving the government greater control over industrial investment and of cutting out the middleman in regulated sectors such as armaments and pharmaceuticals. In addition, he saw nationalisation as providing the government with the means to create model, efficient, innovative and integrated companies, with advanced and co-operative worker-management relations and modern plant and machinery, in key 'leading sector' industries. He aimed to build a nationalised 'economic strike force', able to compete with the most modern American, German and Japanese firms and to play pioneering roles in the growth sectors of computers, biotechnology and microcircuit production.

Twelve industrial groups in all were designated for nationalisation in 1981 and had been earmarked as early as the 1972 'Common Programme'. They included the Dassault and Matra armaments consortia; the Rhône-Poulenc, Roussell-Uclaf and Péchiney-Ugine-Kuhlmann chemical, pharmaceutical and aluminium giants; the troubled Usinor and Sacilor steel groups; the Saint-Gobain industrial combine; the Thomson-Brandt and CGE (*Compagnie Générale d'Électricité*) electrical concerns; and the Cii-Honeywell-Bull and ITT-France computer empires. In addition, 36 of the remaining banks and insurance groups which had escaped nationalisation by de Gaulle in 1944-47 were to be taken into public ownership as a means of better channelling investment in an integrated Japanese-style approach.

The Nationalisation Bill was pioneered through parliament by the moderate Industry Minister Pierre Dreyfus, who sought to reassure the companies being taken over that nationalisation would not mean constant state interference to the detriment of efficiency and initiative. The measure, nevertheless, encountered fierce opposition within the National Assembly and within the conservative Senate, which initially rejected it, and had to be significantly altered after the Constitutional Council declared the bill's compensation terms to be an unconstitutional breach of the 1789 declaration on property rights.[1] It was finally passed, however, in the spring of 1982 and was accompanied by the enactment of the Auroux bill, extending workers' rights within factories, granting unions greater access to company information and formalising annual negotiating arrangements.

These bills represented considerable advances for the French Left, extending workers' rights, almost doubling (from 18% to 32%) the share of industry under public control and bringing the state into important new areas of competitive industrial activity.[2] This first major extension of the public sector since 1947 significantly shifted the balance of the French economy in key sectors and strengthened the state's hand in planning. It was followed by government encouragement of rationalisation and reorganisation within the new industries under its control, assigning individual corporations specific areas and products on which to concentrate.

[1] Such alterations raised the cost of nationalisation to the state by 28%, or £700m.

[2] The state's share by sector rose as follows: banking from 70% to 95%, electronics and information processing from 0% to 60%, synthetic fibres from 0% to 75%, iron and steel from 1% to 79%, chemicals from 16% to 52% and armaments from 58% to 74%. It should be noted, however, that only the parent companies, not the subsidiaries, of the firms noted above were nationalised. In addition, only five conglomerates, Rhône-Poulenc, Péchiney, Thomson, Saint-Gobain and the CGE, were fully taken into public ownership. For the other companies, a number of which had large foreign shareholdings, the government merely took controlling stakes of 51% or less.

However, change was not sweeping. The newly nationalised firms' existing managers were either retained or replaced by experienced bureaucrats and were given relative freedom of management within the outlines of gereral three- to four-year plans. The change from private to state ownership, also, had little obvious impact upon the conditions of workers employed, to the disappointment of the supporters of *autogestion*.

However, while decentralisation and nationalisation were the two great structural reforms effected by the Mitterrand team, its immediate success and popularity rested less upon these measures than on its handling of the economy and the fate of its emergency recovery programme.

This 'recovery programme' broke away from the liberal and monetarist economics of *Barrisme* and set the French economy on a Keynesian/Rooseveltian course of reflation and increased state planning. It sought to pump-prime the economy out of its depressed condition, seeking initial GNP growth of 3% in 1981 to reverse the upward rise in unemployment. This ambitious programme was enthusiastically implemented during 1981/2 in three stages. Firstly, consumer spending was immediately boosted through the grant of higher welfare payments and minimum wages, while monetary growth restrictions were loosened. Secondly, a major housebuilding drive was launched, 54 000 new civil service jobs created (with promises of 125 000 more), 7 billion francs set aside to help school leavers and 17 billion francs in 'soft loan' credit provided to private industry through the local *Comités Départementaux pour le Financement (Codefis)*. Thirdly, state industrial investment was increased substantially, with priority being given to the new high-technology sector under the direction of Research Minister Jean-Pierre Chevènement. These measures taken together increased public spending by a massive 28% in 1981 to a level of 788 billion francs. They were to be paid for by higher taxes on motorists and smokers, by a new wealth tax on high-income earners and by allowing the public sector deficit to double. It was hoped, however, that before long the boost that these measures would give to private and public sector industrial growth would create a virtuous circle of expanding tax revenues and diminishing unemployment benefit charges.

Unfortunately for the Mitterrand team things did not work out as happily as planned in 1981/2, as a result of adverse domestic and international factors. Domestically, both the Paris *Bourse* (financial market) and *Patronat* (industrialists' federation) were opposed to the new government's economic programme, disliking its lax monetary control, its nationalisation plans and its social, labour and tax reforms which directly added to French industry's already high level of initial costs. The Mitterrand government, on assuming office, thus found itself faced with a sudden collapse in the *Bourse*, a decline in the franc exchange rate and an 'investment strike' by French industrialists. Internationally, the new administration under-estimated the severity of the world economic crisis and the structural problems which faced French industry. They believed, encouraged by contemporary OECD (Organisation for Economic Co-operation and Development) surveys, that the worst of the 1979-81 crisis had passed and that a new expansionary era was commencing. They thus sought to give a lead to other nations through being the first to adopt a determinedly reflationary strategy and hoped that others would follow in a Europe-wide recovery programme. The Socialist administration's optimism proved, however, to be ill-founded. Tight neo-monetarist fiscal policies were being pursued elsewhere in the world economy, leading to high interest rates and a contraction in trade growth, while sharpening competition from the NICs of South-east Asia and the onset of new automated technologies were forcing labour-shedding 'rationalisation' in both old and new industries.

Faced with such adverse domestic and international circumstances the new administration rapidly found its ambitious reflationary programme moving out of control. Its boost to demand was initially greeted with public and trade union enthusiasm in what became known as the 'state of grace' during its first six months in office. The hoped-for expansion in exports and industrial output failed, however, to materialise. Thus, by October 1981 the government was faced with the unhappy conjunction of unemployment moving towards two million, inflation rising above 15%, interest rates at 16-18% and a widening trade and budget deficit. The Economy and Finance Minister, Jacques Delors, attempted to stabilise the situation by devaluing the franc, shelving a number of public spending programmes and by imposing a temporary and voluntary prices and wages freeze. Matters, however, continued to deteriorate during the following year as industrial investment and production slumped, forcing more than 20 000 firms into bankruptcy, the nationalised industries into deficit and unemployment to a level in excess of two million. This was accompanied by a dramatic decline in support for the government, though not yet for President Mitterrand himself, which was reflected by losses in the

January and March by-elections and cantonal elections, and by increased unrest among trade unionists, farmers and small shopkeepers. The government responded to these mounting problems by imposing a second currency devaluation, a statutory four-month prices and wages freeze and a package of spending cuts in June 1982. Within the administration, however, major divisions were emerging between radicals and moderates over the correct way forward, preparing the ground for a sudden rethink and U-turn in economic strategy.

President Mitterrand had never shown any great interest in economic affairs but had been attracted by the futuristic state technology visions of radicals such as Attali, Chevènement and Laurent Fabius and had been determined to fulfil his pledge to reduce unemployment. He thus gave full support to the reflationary programme during 1981, only allowing for a minor adjustment in October. By 1982. however, he had become concerned at the high financial cost of the 'reflation in one country' strategy. It had kept the rate of increase in the French unemployment rate below the EEC average and had saved over 100 000 jobs. At the same time, however, it had led to a dangerously widening disparity between the inflation rate of France and its neighbours and a huge growth in external indebtedness which imperilled continued French membership of the EMS. This pressed the President closer to the 'realists' within the cabinet — Delors, Rocard, Jobert and Dreyfus — and persuaded him to call for an easing of the pace of reform in the summer of 1982. Determined not to allow the budget deficit to rise above the figure of 3% of GDP, Mitterrand gave full support to the Delors package of spending cuts in June 1982 and called on government ministers to concentrate henceforth on consolidation rather than radical reform in what he termed the 'second phase of change'.

This switch of course angered the radical 'maximalists', led by Chevènement and Questiaux (Social Services), who boasted the support of a majority of Socialist Party deputies within the National Assembly. They argued, in a manner similar to Britain's Labour Party Bennites during the 1976 IMF (International Monetary Fund) crisis, for an intensification of the reflationary programme with the imposition, if need be, of a number of protectionist controls to enable French industry to 'reconquer the home market'. Failing to move Mitterrand in June 1982, Nicole Questiaux resigned from the cabinet as a mark of opposition.[1] This proved, however, only to be a

---

[1] Pierre Bérégovoy took over Questiaux's portfolio, with Jacques Attali becoming the new Élysée Palace chief of staff.

preliminary test before the final showdown between the 'maximalists' and 'realists' in March 1983.

From June 1982 *rigueur* (austerity) became the watchword for the Mitterrand administration, with top priority being placed upon reducing the rate of inflation to a hoped-for level of 8% by the end of 1983. Tight control was thus maintained over state spending, particularly public sector salary bills and welfare programmes, with the new Social Services Minister, Pierre Bérégovoy, emerging as a tough-minded axe-wielder. Government control was also maintained over prices and wages within closely defined limits, These measures proved insufficient, however, rapidly to redress the nation's trade balance and budget deficit. A third currency devaluation had to be effected and a major deflationary 'austerity programme' introduced in March 1983. This aimed directly at contracting internal demand by 2% through reducing the level of subsidies to nationalised industries, cutting the welfare budget, raising public sector charges and indirect taxes and introducing a special income tax surcharge.

These 'March measures' were carried out following a disastrous performance by the Left in municipal elections which led to a large-scale ministerial reshuffle in which Jean-Pierre Chevènement was replaced as Industry Minister by Laurent Fabius and Jacques Delors added the Budget to his Economy and Finance portfolios.[1] They marked the end of the Socialists' reflationary experiment and represented a return to the fiscal austerity of the Barre years in what was a humbling U-turn for the new administration. From March 1983 onwards the Mitterrand team was to concentrate upon narrowing the trade and budget deficits and bringing down inflation in a Giscardian financier manner. It was also to begin to actively encourage industrial investment through the grant of special concessions and to refuse to constantly prop up 'lame duck' industries with state subsidies. The Mitterrand government did still retain a commitment to strong state planning and state industrial and research investment, but this was only to be within the framework of a sensible annual budget.

This swing towards conservatism was also mirrored in other policy areas after 1982. For example, the Mitterrand administration,

---

[1] Ten ministries were moved out of the cabinet during this reshuffle. In addition, Michel Rocard was transferred to the Agriculture portfolio and Jacques Attali became *conseiller spécial* (special adviser) to the President, his close friend Jean-Louis Bianco replacing him as Élysée chief of staff.

immediately on assuming power, announced plans to freeze the nuclear power programme (cancelling the Plogoff generator project in Brittany) prior to a referendum, and to curb arms sales overseas. By 1983, however, persuaded that these industries provided 500 000 jobs as well as valuable foreign currency earnings, it rescinded these decisions and sanctioned expansion instead. The administration also failed to press through fully with its proposed sweeping reduction in the working week to 35 hours or to establish powerful and influential workers' councils as a result of the opposition from the CNPF (*Conseil National du Patronat Français*) employers' federation, which it was now seeking to court, and, prompted by concern at the mounting level of terrorism and violent crime, stiffened its approach to law and order. Only in the sphere of broadcasting was the reform momentum of 1981 maintained, with the establishment in September 1982 of a new nine-member professional State Broadcasting Authority (SBA) to appoint TV channel heads and establish programme standards and rules.[1]

From Reform to Realism: 1983 — 1986

From the spring of 1983 the Mitterrand administration turned from being one of reform to one of management and consolidation. The President, who had previously occupied an ambiguous position between the radical CERES faction 'maximalists' and the moderate party 'realists', now fully aligned himself with the latter grouping and set about constructing a new and responsible centre-left coalition based around the key figures of Delors, Bérégovoy and Fabius. He projected himself in true presidential fashion as a supra-party, statesmanlike leader who, although forced to change course, was pursuing the only sensible economic strategy available. He now abandoned his 1981 pledge to keep unemployment below two million and devoted himself to a new mission to see French industry modernised and made competitive with world leaders in Japan, Germany and the United States. This would involve major restructuring, technological investment and labour rationalisation,

---

[1]   The new SBA's members were each elected three at a time at triennial intervals to serve nine-year terms. They were appointed on a similar system to the Constitutional Council — three each being selected by the President, National Assembly president (Louis Fermaz) and Senate president (Alain Poher) — giving the authority an initial left-of-centre bias, although it was supposed to be an independent body.

but would be presided over in a humane fashion with the state closely involved in a 'mixed economy' manner. The President sought through this policy approach to undercut his critics in the Right Coalition, who called for a similar, and in many ways harsher, restructuring strategy. He buttressed this firm new approach with the adoption of a more forceful and interventionist stance in foreign affairs, unveiling a major new arms modernisation programme in April 1983 and despatching French peacekeeping troops to Lebanon and Chad (August 1983).

Such a change in strategy failed, however, to satisfy the French public, which turned against the government and parties of the Left in local elections and opinion polls during 1983 and 1984. Indeed, by the autumn of 1983 President Mitterrand's popularity rating, which had reached 60% in March 1982, had slumped to only 30-35%, the lowest level recorded by a President in the history of the Fifth Republic. Matters worsened during the spring of 1984 as economic growth faltered and as the adverse initial effects of the government's restructuring and deflationary programme sent unemployment spiralling. Farmers protested vigorously against low purchase prices; shipbuilders, car workers, coal miners and steelworkers sporadically went on strike in opposition to plant closures; civil servants demonstrated against the government's pay restraint policy; and lorry drivers paralysed the nation's road network in remonstration against customs delays and taxes. This 'spring of discontent' was made even more serious by the recrudescence of the inflammatory and divisive issues of immigration and church education.

Racist feeling, which had been evident between 1979-81, was revived in France by the mounting level of unemployment, which led to calls for the forced repatriation of the almost two million immigrant workers from Algeria, Morocco and Tunisia who were particularly prominent in the country's troubled motor industry. The Mitterrand administration responded to this change in public mood by introducing tighter controls against illegal immigration in 1983. This failed, however, to check the alarming increase in racially motivated violence and the rise in public support for the neo-fascist National Front in local elections, which threatened to endanger the nation's stability and unity.

France's venerable secular-clerical divisions, which had lain largely dormant for decades, were reopened by the plans of the Mitterrand administration to exert firmer state control over private, mostly Roman Catholic, schools or else cease their funding. These 'free church schools', to which a sixth of French school pupils were sent, boasted a higher standard of education than ordinary state schools, receiving funds, as they did, from both parents and the state, and were opposed as the reactionary and élitist schools of the rich by the parties of the Left. Particularly critical were the FEN state teachers' union and freemasons, who provided respectively a half and a quarter of Socialist Party deputies in the 1981-86 parliament. They sought the establishment of a single state lay educational system, as had been promised by François Mitterrand during the 1981 presidential campaign. Once in government, however, President Mitterrand and his Education Minister Alain Savary tried to put together a compromise solution which would appeal to both Left and Right, but succeeded only in provoking the opposition of both groups. As the new education bill neared completion a series of mass rallies were organised in Rennes, Lille, Versailles and Paris in February-June 1984, attracting combined crowds of more than two million. Right-wing groups attempted to make use of this anti-secular feeling in a destabilising campaign against the government.

At the height of these troubles, the Mitterrand administration was forced to undergo a national test of its popularity in the new elections to the European Parliament on 17 June 1984. Faced with working-class resentment of social spending cuts and middle-class opposition to recent tax increases, the Socialist Party's vote declined dramatically from its 1981 Assembly election high of 38% to only 21%. Support for the Socialists' government partners, the PCF, slumped similarly from 16% to only 11%. Unfortunately, however, for the parties of the Right Coalition, who had grouped themselves together for this election under the leadership of the former EEC president Simone Veil and who had looked upon June as a plebiscite on the government's record, it was not they who benefited from the swing away from the left. Support for the RPR-UDF combined ticket rose only 3% above its June 1981 level to 43%. It was, rather, the extreme, racist right, in the form of Jean-Marie Le Pen's National Front, which proved to be most successful in the June Euro-elections, its vote soaring to 11%, enabling it to capture European Assembly seats for the first time ever.[1]

---

[1] The PS captured 20 seats in this election, the PCF 10, the RPR-UDF 41 and the National Front 10. It should be noted, however, that the electoral turnout was only 57%, many supporters of the 'conventional' Right and Left abstaining.

Although the verdict of the June 1984 Euro-elections was not as clear and damning as the Mitterrand government may have feared, it was sufficient to persuade the President that a major ministerial reshuffle and policy reappraisal was required if party fortunes were to improve in time for the vital 1986 Assembly elections. President Mitterrand decided, moreover, that in this reshuffle change had to begin at the top with the replacement of his Prime Minister, Pierre Mauroy. Mauroy had proved to be a loyal, efficient and dedicated servant to the President, but, although trying hard to adapt himself to the 'new realism' and austerity of the Mitterrand administration, appeared increasingly as an anachronistic figure. He remained trapped in the rhetoric of traditional 'big spending' socialism and was not fully committed to the job-shedding rationalisation called for under the changed circumstances of 1984-86. In addition, his health was deteriorating. Mauroy was thus relieved of his post as Prime Minister in July 1984. His replacement was the 37-year-old Industry Minister Laurent Fabius, an *énarque* technocrat and former financial servant who was the son of a wealthy, Jewish Paris art dealer and who enjoyed a firm political base in the Rouen region. Fabius' promotion at such a young age was a surprise, but he had worked closely with Mitterrand as an economic adviser since 1976 and was a driving force behind the new rationalisation and modernisation strategy. He was an engagingly popular moderate 'social democrat' who would give the administration a more youthful and dynamic image.

Fabius' influence over economic affairs was further strengthened by the departure of Jacques Delors to Brussels to take over the presidency of the EEC Commission. Delors, who had been tipped as a possible prime ministerial choice himself and who had been the architect of the 1982-84 austerity programme, was replaced in the key Economy, Finance and Budget Ministry by the Social Affairs Minister Pierre Bérégovoy. Bérégovoy, a close ally of President Mitterrand, was a self-made man — a café-owner's son who had worked his way up from the shopfloor to become a state industrial manager — who contrasted sharply in background to the upper bourgeoisie Fabius. He shared, however, a similar economic outlook and was to work closely with Fabius and the Industry Minister Edith Cresson (50) as part of a troika in charge of economic policy.

The new ministerial team of 17 (see Table 10) included two other significant changes. Firstly, Gaston Defferre was replaced at the Interior Ministry by the leftist, former party Assembly leader, Pierre

Joxe (49): Defferre now took over the Planning/Regional Development portfolio. Second, and more importantly, Jean-Pierre Chevènement replaced Alain Savary at Education in what heralded a dramatic policy U-turn. Savary had resigned from his post in July 1984 after President Mitterrand, shocked by the events of February-June 1984, decided not to ratify the June 1984 education bill which had sought to cut the funding of those private schools which refused to yield to state control. The President gave his replacement, the rehabilitated CERES leader Chevènement (44), himself the son of a teacher, the brief to effect a compromise deal which would heal the party's rift with the church education lobby and to concentrate on raising general school standards and instilling discipline and a new 'republican patriotism'.

TABLE 10 : LEADING POSTS IN THE MITTERRAND CABINET OF JULY 1984

Laurent Fabius	Prime Minister[1]	Michel Delebarre	Labour[2]
Pierre Bérégovoy	Economy, Finance & Budget[1]	Htte Bouchardeau	Environment[1]
		Hubert Curien	Research & Techn.[2]
Edith Cresson	Industry & For. Trade[1]	Roland Dumas	European Affairs
Pierre Joxe	Interior & Decentr.[2]	Michel Crepeau	Commerce & Tourism
Robert Badinter	Justice	Paul Quiles	Housing & Transport
Gaston Defferre	Planning & Reg. Dev.[1]	Charles Hernu	Defence
Claude Cheysson	External Relations	Michel Rocard	Agriculture
J-P Chevènement	Education[3]	Georgina Dufoix	Social Affairs[1]

[1] Given New Post   [2] New To Cabinet   [3] Returning to Cabinet

The major development in July 1984 was, however, the PCF's decision to withdraw its ministers from the new government as a means of displaying opposition to the new job-shedding deflationary economic strategy. Such a breach had long been anticipated ever since the June 1982 package of cuts, but had been delayed for tactical reasons and as a result of internal policy disputes. The move did not mean that Communist deputies would vote against the government on confidence motions (they would in fact abstain). It did, however, mean that the Mitterrand administration would in future face growing criticism from its PCF left flank, as well as the possibility of serious industrial unrest from an unleashed CGT.

The new Fabius administration, shorn of PCF participation, sought to project itself as a more determinedly centrist force than the preceding Mauroy government. It continued to give top priority to the fight against inflation and proceeded to introduce a series of

83

tough budgetary packages aimed at eliminating waste in the public sector. It, secondly, stressed the need for industrial modernisation and retraining. It, thirdly, zealously pushed through a series of new liberal free-market economic initiatives which reflected contemporary 'social democratic' thinking. These included a lowering of income and company tax levels in the budgets for 1985 and 1986; a reduction in state interference in nationalised industry planning and management; the deregulation of a number of industrial and consumer prices (including that of petrol); the relaxation of exchange controls; and the sanctioning of the privatisation of profitable subsidiaries of nationalised firms and the raising of capital for nationalised firms through the issue of special investment bonds. This new deregulatory and more market-centred policy approach was supported in the political sphere by the slow and continuing devolution of funds and powers from central to local tiers of government and by the lifting of the state television monopoly.[1]

This new, reformist, policy approach was greeted with initial public enthusiasm and brought a number of tangible achievements. The French inflation rate was gradually brought down to a level of 5%, with wage increases falling similarly; the trade deficit was reduced substantially and the budget deficit held at 3% of GDP; the franc exchange rate was stabilised; interest rates were slowly reduced to only 10%; nationalised industries began to return to profit; and private sector industrial investment picked up after the slump of 1982-84. Unfortunately, however, for the new administration one economic index failed to improve, that of unemployment. 1984/5 saw instead a major surge in its level, breaching the 2.5 million mark in November 1984, before settling at a proportionate rate of 10.8%. This unemployment was partly 'structural', being caused by industrial 'rationalisation' as French firms installed new automated technology and replaced manpower to raise labour productivity. It also resulted, however, from French firms' continued problems of international competitiveness, which led to company bankruptcy rates in excess of 24 000 per annum, and the government's unwillingness to 'bale out' troubled concerns.[2]

[1] The first private TV franchise was given to a pro-Socialist Italian-French consortium which began broadcasting in February 1986.

[2] The most striking example of the Fabius government's new hard-nosed attitude towards business failures was its decision in December 1984 to allow the bankrupt Creusot-Loire engineering giant to enter receivership.

The Fabius administration's economic record thus proved to be chequered. The government continued to pay the price for the costly reflationary experiment of 1981/2 which limited the fiscal room for manoeuvre between 1984-86. Thus, during these years both the French inflation and industrial growth rates were inferior to those of its competitors in Japan, Germany and the United States. France's unemployment rate still remained somewhat below the EEC and OECD average. This was, however, little consolation to a public which was shocked by the high level of youth unemployment (25% of 16-24-year-olds being without work) and by the novel phenomenon of the *nouveaux pauvres*, a term which referred to the 150 000-500 000 long-term unemployed who were forced to sleep rough and feed at soup kitchens as a result of financial hardship. It was no surprise, therefore, to see the popularity rating of President Mitterrand slump below 30% in the autumn of 1984 and that of the Socialist Party fall to a level of only 25%.

This low rating for the President and Socialist Party was confirmed by the important test of the cantonal elections of March 1985. With half the French electorate eligible to vote, the Socialist-MRG grouping secured only 26.5% of the total vote and the PCF a mere 12.7%. The RPR-UDF Right opposition parties captured, by contrast, 49% of the vote and gained control of 69 of the country's 96 département councils: the far-right National Front garnered a further 8.7% of the vote. It was a disastrous performance for the parties of the Left and persuaded President Mitterrand that changes had to be made if an RPR-UDF parliamentary landslide was to be averted in the crucial March 1986 National Assembly elections. He ruled out, however, any major change in economic policy, believing that the year ahead would slowly see some returns emerging from the 1983-86 austerity programme. The President instead determined upon constitutional reform, pushing through the thirteenth change in the nation's electoral laws since the advent of adult male suffrage in 1848, with the switch from the first-past-the-post two-ballot system to one of proportional representation (PR) based on département level party lists.

The switch to PR was not a sudden decision. It had, in fact, been a long-cherished goal of the French Left, who viewed the Gaullist Fifth Republic first-past-the-post system as unjust to minor and opposition parties, and had formed one of the '110 Proposals for Change' presented by François Mitterrand to the French electorate during the presidential race of 1981. Its implementation in April 1985 was, however, strongly influenced by narrow and opportunistic party political considerations. This became clear as polling agency and Interior Department computers began to make projections which showed conclusively that without PR the Socialist Party would face such a crushing parliamentary defeat that the President would be turned into a 'lame duck' prisoner of the Right Coalition. By contrast, these studies predicted that with a party list version of PR the Socialists would retain a substantial bloc within the National Assembly and could look forward to small Centre groups and the far-right National Front eating into the RPR-UDF vote, minimising the scale of defeat and even creating the possibility of the construction of a new ad hoc centre-left coalition. PR was thus desperately grasped as the potential saviour of the Mitterrand presidency after 1986. Its introduction was, not surprisingly therefore, strongly opposed by the parties of the Right Coalition. They declared that it would threaten a return to the political instability and fragmented backroom politics of the Fourth Republic, would sever the traditional constituency links of deputies and would bring into the Assembly representatives of the racist National Front. They portrayed the move as one of brutal and cynical *charcutage* (electoral butchery), but were powerless to prevent the passage of the bill by the Socialist-controlled National Assembly on 10 April 1985.[1]

The Mitterrand administration would need to wait a year before judgement could be passed on the wisdom of this reform. The government paid, however, an immediate price for passage of the measure in the resignation of Agriculture Minister Michel Rocard, who was opposed to the change, viewing it as a threat to 'firm and efficient' government. Rocard, who had felt aggrieved at not being offered the prestigious Finance portfolio in July 1984 and who had presidential ambitions for 1988, in many respects used the PR issue as a useful one on which to resign. His resignation was nevertheless a serious loss for the Mitterrand-Fabius government, robbing it of an immensely popular and respected figure who would now feel free to launch damaging attacks from outside its ranks.

More unexpected problems for the administration in the run-up to the vital March 1986 National Assembly elections were provided by events in the remote South Pacific.

---

[1] The rule change included a 5% threshold level for representation and the allocation of seats according to the 'highest average system'. To accommodate it, the number of seats in the National Assembly was expanded from 491 to 577. The bill became law on 26 June 1985 when it passed through the National Assembly for the third time, thus overruling the rejections of the Senate.

In the small island dependency of New Caledonia, a violent separatist struggle which developed between indigenous Kanaks and local French settlers provoked a series of fierce parliamentary battles between the Mitterrand government, who favoured granting independence to the island, and Jacques Chirac's RPR, who sided with the settler community. It rekindled some of the divisions of the Algerian war years and led to government clashes with the Constitutional Council and taunts from the Right Opposition that the President was seeking to 'sell out' French interests overseas.

It was, however, the 'Rainbow Warrior Affair', which dominated French politics between August and October 1985, which promised to be more directly damaging to the government, leading as it did to the enforced resignation of Defence Minister Charles Hernu and tarnishing the reputations of Prime Minister Fabius and the President himself. The affair centred around the mining of the Greenpeace flagship, the Rainbow Warrior, in Auckland harbour on 10 July 1985, which resulted in the death of one crew member. The environmental action group's boat had been in New Zealand preparing to voyage to the Mururoa atoll region of the South Pacific to protest against French nuclear tests due to commence in October 1985. It emerged that those involved in the mining had been French DGSE (*Direction Générale da la Sécurité Extérieure*) secret service agents determined to frustrate this mission. At first it was thought that the action had been undertaken without authorisation by far-right freebooters within the DGSE. Gradually, however, investigative journalism by the French press, with *Le Monde* taking the lead, uncovered an unseemly web which suggested that the action had been given high official sanction.

The administration tried at first to brush away the crisis by sanctioning a short inquiry by Bernard Tricot, an old adviser to General de Gaulle, which uncovered little. This failed, however, to placate the media, parliamentary opposition and French public. A second and more intensive inquiry was thus launched in September 1985, which finally came to the conclusion that the Rainbow Warrior mining had been officially sanctioned. As a consequence, Defence Minister, Charles Hernu, and the DGSE chief, Admiral Pierre Lacoste, resigned on 20 September, although the former protested that he had merely sanctioned a reconnaissance mission, not a mining. These resignations brought an end to the unsavoury affair but failed to fully clear up the mystery and establish the true role of the army and DGSE.

The Rainbow Warrior incident did not prove to be as damaging for the Mitterrand administration as might have seemed likely. The majority of the French public favoured a strong foreign policy approach, supported nuclear tests in the South Pacific and opposed the Greenpeace environmentalist movement. They did believe, however, that the mining of an unprotected vessel went beyond the bounds of acceptable behaviour and disliked the reticence of the administration. The affair did not, therefore, help the troubled Mitterrand government as it approached the March 1986 elections and made the prospect of the Socialist Party retaining a parliamentary majority increasingly remote.

The March 1986 National Assembly Elections

The slump in the fortunes of the Left registered in the opinion polls, by-elections and local elections during the years after its June 1981 triumph made defeat in the crucial March 1986 National Assembly elections virtually certain. Two telling illustrations of the Left's demise were the facts that prior to June 1981 the Socialist Party and PCF controlled 42 of the country's 96 département councils and 159 of its 221 municipalities with a population in excess of 30 000. By March 1986 the Left's share of the former had been reduced to 26 and of the latter to 128. The parties of the Right were thus now clearly dominant at the local government level, their ideology was in the ascendant and they appeared poised to regain control over the central levers of power. Only the exact scale of the Right Coalition's victory and the designation of its new Prime Minister remained unclear, being influenced by inter-party developments and by shorter-term factors as the campaign for the March elections moved underway.

Divisions within the Right Coalition

The dominant personality in the Right Coalition by March 1986 was the RPR leader and former Prime Minister Jacques Chirac (53). He had emerged as the key 'fixer' within the coalition as early as June 1981 and as its principal parliamentary spokesman in the succeeding years. He had also kept himself in the public eye as an innovative Mayor of Paris, pushing through major housebuilding, urban renewal and cultural programmes to revive once declining inner city areas. Chirac had, thirdly and most importantly, established firm control over the organisation and ideology of the RPR. He installed his forceful protégé, Jacques Toubon (44), a Paris casino croupier's son, as secretary-general in 1984, to set about improving the local grass-roots RPR machine, building up membership to a level of 740 000, the highest of any French political party. Meanwhile, Chirac remoulded and updated the RPR's policy outlook, moving it decisively away from traditional 'one nation', state interventionist Gaullism towards a neo-liberal, 'new right' Reaganite-Thatcherite policy programme. Thus in domestic affairs Chirac and the RPR now pressed for tax and public spending cuts, denationalisation, deregulation and reduced government interference with the aim of encouraging a new individualist and enterprise spirit. In foreign affairs, while continuing to favour a strongly independent and nationalistic stance, Chirac similarly moved away from traditional Gaullism in stressing fierce opposition to the Soviet Union and the importance of good transatlantic relations with America, and he emerged as a 'born again' advocate of a more co-operative approach within the European Community, although determined still to uphold French farm interests.

Chirac, with this policy approach, established himself as the most conspicuous politician within the conventional French Right during the years between 1981 and 1984. He remained, however, a controversial figure who, with his impetuous, opportunistic, rabble-rousing style and his tendency to attach himself to extremist issues such as immigrant repatriation and anti-abortion, was either loved or hated. Chirac thus drew support from a narrower, though more committed, base than other party leaders within the Right Coalition, thus imperilling his prospects of emerging as Prime Minister in 1986 or President in 1988. Recognising this, Chirac, influenced by a clutch of new public relations advisers, attempted to soften his style in the period immediately before March 1986. He adopted a more restrained, conciliatory and statesmanlike posture during, for example, the 'Rainbow Warrior Affair', and he engaged in frequent, high-profile overseas visits. This change in style proved, however, to be a twin-edged sword, improving Chirac's credibility as a national leader, but losing him the support of far-right zealots to the emerging National Front. In the meantime, Chirac was also faced with growing competition from his two rivals in the Right Coalition, Giscard d'Estaing and Raymond Barre, both of whom indirectly attached themselves to the UDF and appealed for moderate conservative support.

The former President Valéry Giscard d'Estaing (60) proved to be less of a threat to Chirac than Raymond Barre. He maintained a low profile during the first two years of the Mitterrand presidency and left control of the amorphous UDF grouping to its president, Jean Lecanuet, paying little attention to the improvement of its organisational structure. He retained, however, ambitions of recovering the presidency in 1988, and slowly began to re-enter the political scene, regaining his département council and National Assembly seats in the Auvergne and Puy-de-Dôme with huge majorities in March 1982 and September 1984. As Giscard slowly cast off what he termed his 'widower's weeds', he became increasingly critical of the Mitterrand administration, presenting himself once more as the natural leader of the moderate and liberal 'new centre'. He put forward a policy programme combining the Chiraquian themes of tax cuts, deregulation and privatisation with a more liberal and humane approach to social issues and attempted to portray himself once more as a common, down-to-earth man of the people, hoping to attract disillusioned Socialist voters to his banner. Such an approach failed, however, to engage the French public, who continued to recall the haughty, regal Giscard of the 1976-81 period, and who viewed the former President as yesterday's man. In addition, Giscard's standing was undermined in 1983 and 1984 by newspaper revelations and a government report which showed that, between 1974-81, President Giscard and the state-owned oil company, Elf-Aquitaine, had been duped of £65 million through the foolhardy funding of an Italian scientist who claimed to have invented an aeroplane capable of 'sniffing out' possible underground oil deposits.

With Giscard failing to make headway in the years between 1984 and 1986, it was his former Prime Minister, Raymond Barre (61), who emerged as the chief challenger to Jacques Chirac within the Right Coalition and who even began to outscore Chirac in national opinion polls. This change in fortune was surprising for a man who had been a most unpopular figure between 1979 and 1981 and who lacked a party base of his own, standing as an independent with only the most cursory ties to the UDF. It was brought about by the failed Socialist reflationary experiment of 1981/2, which Barre had continuously criticised as dangerously wrong-headed in the columns of the liberal-conservative magazine *L'Express*, and by President Mitterrand's U-turn towards austerity and market forces from the spring of 1983. This was taken as a vindication of the economic approach of Raymond Barre, whose two-volume textbook *Economic Policy* now became essential reading on campuses across the country, and of his period in office between 1976-81. Barre now became viewed as a man of steadfastness and integrity who had been right all along. In addition, he attracted the support of traditional UDF and RPR conservatives who disapproved of either the social liberalism of Giscard or the extremist posturing of Chirac. He began to build up a strong power base in the Lyons area and was given media backing by the influential press baron Robert Hersant, who disliked both Giscard and Chirac.

The National Front: A New 'Flash Party' from the Right

The great threat to the parties of the 'Conventional Right', however, in March 1986 was the sudden emergence of the extreme right, racist National Front. This party first rose to prominence during the September 1983 municipal election, when it captured 17% of the vote in Dreux near Paris, and during the Euro-election of June 1984 and local cantonal elections of March 1985 it secured, on a national basis, a surprising 10.5% of the vote. It represented the latest example of one of the many 'flash parties' which have briefly emerged in French history, and it drew deeply on a latent reservoir of popular racism, which had been evident in the 1890s during the Dreyfus affair and during the 1930s and 1940s Vichy period, and more tangentially on the extra-parliamentary activities of ultra-rightist extremist groups such as the SAC (Civic Action Service) and FANE (the Federation for National and European Action).

The background to the emergence of the National Front was provided by the renaissance of 'new right' élitist and Euro-centric intellectual thinking pioneered by the young philosopher Alain de Benoist in the journals of the *Figaro Magazine* during 1979 and by the outbreak of a series of violent terrorist attacks directed at Jewish and North African groups during 1980 and 1982. It was, however, the sharp rise in unemployment after 1980 which turned the 'immigrant question' into a burning issue and vitalised the fortunes of the National Front.[1] The party had been established in 1972 by

---

[1] France's immigrant community numbered 4.5 million in 1982: 8% of the total population. This compared with figures of 5% and 6% for the UK and West Germany. 34% of these immigrants were drawn from North Africa, 20% from Portugal and 10% each from Italy and Spain.

Jean-Marie Le Pen, a former law student and paratrooper who first rose to prominence as a young deputy for the Poujadist 'flash party' in 1956 and who fought to keep Algeria French during the later 1950s, losing an eye during a violent street battle. It adopted a fiercely nationalistic and anti-communist line in foreign affairs; called for a return to traditional family values and a sterner approach to law and order, favouring restoration of the death penalty; and pressed for an abolition of income and wealth taxes and the replacement of the state social security system with private insurance schemes. It was, however, the National Front's vocal and controversial stance on immigration which attracted the greatest attention. It charged the nation's North African immigrant community with seeking to establish an Islamic hegemony on French soil and of being a drain on social security revenues, the cause of white unemployment and the key factor in the rise in the violent crime and terrorism rate. The party criticised the Mitterrand administration for wrong-headed liberalism when dealing with the immigrant issue and called for the introduction of an immediate programme of compulsory repatriation. This simplistic message was aggressively delivered by Le Pen and his party supporters and found a responsive chord among indigenous professional and blue-collar workers in the southern Midi region and northern cities, where North African immigration was most concentrated, during 1984 and 1985. [1]

The National Front's sources of support and policy programme differed substantially from those of the Poujadists between 1956-58: the latter represented a rural and provincial-based party of shopkeepers and small businessmen protesting against economic modernisation and growing state control. It was similar, however, in the narrowness of its appeal and in representing a catchment for protest votes cast by former supporters of the RPR and PCF. Similarly, the National Front, while boasting tangential support from local notables and from right-wing elements within the police, army and media, remained an outcast party for the French political establishment. [2] Thus the RPR and UDF, though briefly allying with

[1] In parts of the Marseilles Midi region the party drew in local support of almost 30%.

[2] The Mitterrand government was forced to dismiss the Paris police chief and the director-general of the national police after 2500 Paris policemen joined Le Pen in plain clothes to protest outside the office of Justice Minister Badinter in June 1983.

the party at Dreux in September 1983, refused to engage in any second ballot or coalition pact with the National Front in the years after 1984. This limited the party's ability to translate its voting strength into actual seats: the National Front capturing only one out of the 2000 département council seats at stake during the March 1985 local elections. However, with the introduction of PR, the National Front looked forward to making a substantial impact in March 1986, seeking to possibly hold the balance of power in the new National Assembly.

The Left Coalition Prepares for Defeat

While the parties in the Right Coalition were resurgent between 1982 and 1985 and jockeyed for leadership and control of the French polity in 1986, the Left Coalition parties were demoralised by successive electoral setbacks and contemplated humbling defeat in the forthcoming National Assembly elections.

It was surprisingly, however, the PCF, the junior partner in the government coalition, which was worst affected during this period. The decline in its fortunes, which had been clearly evident between 1979 and 1981, continued steadily during the first five years of the Mitterrand presidency, with the party's support slumping from a national level of 16% to one of only 12%, further eroding its municipal and local government base. The PCF was also damaged and divided by the peculiar nature of its pact with the Mitterrand government between 1981 and 1984. Its government ministers, particularly Transport Minister Charles Fiterman, loyally adhered to the government line, while those outside, particularly secretary-general Georges Marchais, *L'Humanité* editor Roland Leroy and Assembly leader André Lajoinie, fiercely criticised government domestic and foreign policies. They supported a staunch 'Moscow line' over Poland, backing Jaruzelski's December 1981 military crackdown; opposed President Mitterrand's approval of the stationing of American nuclear missiles in Europe; and criticised Delors' budget cutbacks, calling instead for continuing economic reflation. This willingness to be a member of, while continuously criticising, a government created confusion among PCF supporters. Meanwhile its continued subservience to Moscow over foreign policy issues, particularly Poland, forfeited the PCF public support and exacerbated divisions between party reformers and traditionalists.

By the spring of 1983, the PCF leadership was in such a confused and uncertain condition that it proved unable to bring itself to break its pact with the Mitterrand government despite the sharp U-turn that was taking place in economic policy. When the party did finally withdraw its ministers in July 1984, it proved to be too late to rally back lost support. A hardline, traditionalist policy line was adopted at the PCF's 25th Congress in January 1985, with reformist members such as Pierre Juquin and Marcel Rigout being forced into the background, and the CGT was encouraged to foment labour unrest. Voters and workers failed, however, to respond to this policy change. The PCF thus entered the March 1986 elections in a disturbed and debilitated condition. Party membership had plummeted as its blue-collar, peasant farmer and middle-class professional bases of support had been either eroded by recession or been weaned away by the Socialist Party, while many of its younger supporters had transferred their allegiance to the more active National Front and RPR. Its base of support was thus aging and shrinking, a phenomenon which was even visible in its bedrock areas: the party now only controlled, for example, 39 of the 123 municipal councils in the once solidly communist 'red belt' around Paris. In such circumstances the PCF was grateful for the introduction of proportional representation in the March 1986 National Assembly elections. It still faced, however, the possible humiliation of finishing behind the emergent National Front in fifth place as the elections approached.

The Socialist Party remained, by contrast, a powerful political force despite the electoral setbacks it had experienced between 1982-85. It had lost the support of many first-time voters drawn to the party in 1981, who had been disillusioned by its subsequent record in office. However, it boasted a firm local base, the allegiance of a young, new generation of political leaders and activists and, with the support of a quarter of the French electorate, could rightly claim to be the single most popular party in France. The problem for the PS was rather one of strategy as it sought to determine the best way forward in the new and changed political circumstances. It had established itself as the dominant party on the Left, but appeared unable to gain a parliamentary majority in March 1986 standing alone or in combination with the PCF. The question thus emerged, whether it should change its approach and seek out allies in the Centre of French politics, uniting around a new 'social democratic' programme.

The principal advocate of the latter, 'Republican Front', strategy was Michel Rocard. He believed that the party should come to terms with the policy changes it had effected in government since June 1982, renounce its traditionalist call for a 'break with capitalism', firmly close the door on any future pacts or alliances with the PCF, and clearly adopt a new policy programme which embraced market forces, concentrated attention upon the quest for economic modernisation and welcomed the support of like-minded Centrist groupings. Such a strategy was not, surprisingly, opposed by the CERES left wing of the party, who abhorred the 1982-86 policy U-turns of the Mitterrand government and who remained the keenest advocates of alliance with the PCF. It was also, however, rejected by the dominant Mitterrandiste core of the party, led by the Protestant former college professor Lionel Jospin, first-secretary of the PS since 1981. This majority grouping, while accepting the tactical policy-trimming of 1982-86, remained committed in the long term to a socialist transformation of French society and were determined to maintain the left-wing identity of the PS, even if this meant enduring a period in opposition.

These differences were kept out of the open during the October 1983 party congress, with all groups agreeing to unite around a bland policy statement supportive of the Mitterrand administration. During 1985, however, a major split developed following Michel Rocard's resignation from the cabinet. Rocard (55), with ambitions of his own for the presidency in 1988, refused to back a 'joint party programme' in advance and pressed instead for the adoption of his 'Republican Front' strategy and a recantment of the 1981/2 'Socialist experiment' by the party congress in October. He also made vigorous efforts to increase his faction's share of party committee posts to a level of 30%.

When the 1400-member, three-day Congress gathered in Toulouse, however, Rocard was to find himself out-manoeuvred by Jospin (48) and the mainstream Mitterrandistes. The latter put forward a motion which forswore traditional Marxist rhetoric and pledged full support for the government's post-1983 policy approach of pragmatic and realistic socialism. This modernised policy programme was 'social democratic' in nature, thus cutting the ground from under Rocard. The Mitterrandistes refused, however, to sanction future alliances with parties to the right or to fully slam the door on the PCF and communist voters, still viewing the PS, 'the party of the wage-earners', as one historically rooted on the Left. It was a skilful move and won the day following a powerful and rousing speech by Prime Minister Fabius, a man who straddled the

Rocard and Mitterrand camps in outlook, trumpeting the achievements of 1984/5 and calling for all factions within the party to unite around the 'new-look Socialism'. Rocard, whose rambling speech at Toulouse was ill-received, thus decided to relent at the final moment and approved the joint election manifesto on the last day of the Congress, thus averting a damaging split and threatened breakaway.

The Toulouse Congress thus ended in triumph for the *Mitterrandistes*. The price paid, however, was a significant shift towards the centre in the party's policy stance: a shift which may prove, in retrospect, to have been as important as that effected by the German SPD at Bad Godesberg in 1959. The crucial, behind-the-scenes, influence during the Congress was the President himself. He now projected himself as an above-party figure and failed to attend the Congress in person. In reality, however, President Mitterrand had weekly meetings with Jospin and remained in close touch with party affairs. His influence increased between October 1985 and March 1986, as he became unusually closely involved in the crucial National Assembly election campaign.

The Campaign for the March 1986 National Assembly Elections

The campaign for the March 1986 National Assembly elections was peculiarly fierce and protracted. Much was at stake, control of the government and the opportunity to steal a march for the succeeding presidential election, and an unusually powerful, familiar and well-matched sextet of party leaders was contesting for power. The 1986 campaign was also of particular interest and novelty in being the first national parliamentary election for 30 years to be fought under a one-ballot PR system. This forced significant changes in the relationships between the partners and associates within each of the broad Right and Left Coalitions, in methods of candidate selection and in the personalised nature of constituency level contests.

Under the old first-past-the-post, two-ballot electoral system the parties within each of the two major coalitions had been forced to arrange pacts and agreements for each round of the parliamentary contest and the months prior to the elections had been consumed with frantic jockeying as each party leader sought to establish his dominance within the coalition. During the period between·1981 and 1986, the PCF and Socialists had maintained Second Ballot 'stand-down agreements', while the RPR and UDF had put up a united list for the June 1984 Euro-election and had agreed upon joint candidates for more than half the seats contested in local elections. In 1986, with PR, matters changed. Intra-coalition pre-election pacts no longer seemed necessary and were discarded by the Socialists and PCF, who put up separate département lists. Joint lists were also dispensed with by the Right Coalition in 42 of the nation's largest départements, but were retained in smaller, rural départements. Pre-election manoeuvring thus now became concentrated within individual parties as département lists were compiled and attempts were made to harmonise the demands of the centre and the regions in the placement of candidates. Backroom bargains were effected to ensure that intra-party factions were justly represented and a hectic movement, termed *parachutage* (parachuting), of prominent party members from marginal to new safe départements was effected, often to the rancour of displaced local politicians.[1]

Once these lists were agreed, the real campaign for the March 1986 elections moved underway. The parties of the Right Coalition took the lead, issuing a joint, 21-point manifesto for government on 16 January 1986. This represented a compromise document, which dropped a number of the more extreme demands of Jacques Chirac, such as the forced expulsion of unemployed immigrants, the denationalisation of Renault, the prohibition of abortion and the renegotiation of Spanish and Portuguese entry terms to the EEC, and which accepted key social reforms of the Mitterrand administration, for example the 39-hour week, retirement at 60 and the fifth week of paid holiday. It still, however, marked a significant

[1] The problems were especially acute for the Socialist Party, which expected its parliamentary representation to fall from 285 to circa 160-170. Its final lists were drawn up by the PS National Executive Committee in November 1985 and gave each of the party's four main factions a share of winnable seats in proportion to their present strength in the National Assembly: the Mitterrand group was thus given 81 of the top 160 list places, the Mauroyites 29, the Rocardians 28 (a number two below that needed for the formation of a separate, independent party grouping within parliament), the CERES faction 19, non-socialists (for example, Bouchardeau, formerly of the PSU, and Olivier Stirn, formerly of the UDF) 7 and women 9. Agreement was also made with the MRG to run joint lists in 76 *départements*. Within the Right Coalition, the RPR was given higher placements on its joint lists with the UDF, while the press baron, Robert Hersant, succeeded in securing 20 of his employees senior places on the lists. A number of right-wing notables, for example, Marie-France Garaud, ran separate lists, and in all there were 807 lists in France's 96 départements and 7000 candidates: this compared with 2700 candidates in 1981.

break for the Right away from traditional dirigisme towards a new neo-liberal, deregulatory, 'small government' approach, with the document calling for five major changes in the economic sphere: abolition of the wealth tax and reduction of the maximum rate of income tax from 60% to 50%; the immediate scrapping of all remaining price and exchange controls; the denationaliation of banks, insurance companies and industries nationalised by the Mitterrand government; government spending cuts of $10 billion in two years; and an easing of tax burdens and labour restrictions on private companies. In other spheres it called for an abolition of the new PR electoral system, the privatisation of the state television networks, a firmer approach to law and order, including the reintroduction of stop-and-search identity checks, and a repeal of the new 1984 press monopoly law.[1]

However, despite this common manifesto, divisions began to emerge within the Right Coalition once campaigning moved underway, in particular over the issue of what should be done if victory was achieved in March. Chirac and Giscard favoured, in such circumstances, forming a Right Coalition government and drawing as much power away from the hands of the President as possible. They differed, however, over who should become Prime Minister. Raymond Barre, in contrast, refused to countenance *cohabitation* with a Socialist President, believing that President Mitterrand should immediately resign if he lost his Assembly majority and fight a new presidential election. Barre was strongly influenced in adopting this stance by the fact that polls showed that in a snap election he stood the best chance of victory.

These divisions in strategy proved to be deeply damaging for the Right Coalition and particularly for Raymond Barre, whose interpretation of the 1958 constitution appeared flawed and who seemed to be offering the country the prospect of political chaos after March. They gave the opportunity for the Socialist Party to mount a dramatic revival in the polls, putting themselves forward as the party of constitutionality and order. This opportunity was eagerly grasped by President Mitterrand, who emerged to play an active role in the March 1986 election campaign.

[1]   This law had sought to restrict individuals to control of up to 15% of either national or provincial newspaper circulation or 10% of both. It was directed against Robert Hersant, who controlled 30% of national press sales and 26% of provincial, but had proved to be of limited value since the Constitutional Council ruled that it could not be retroactively applied and, in any case, Hersant, as a Euro-MP, was immune from prosecution.

During previous National Assembly elections, the campaign for the incumbent administration had usually been spearheaded by the Prime Minister with the President adopting an aloof, supra-party stance, as befitted his constitutional role as the 'umpire' of the nation. However, during 1973 and 1978, the President, fearing a loss of his coalition's parliamentary majority, had intervened indirectly on television in an attempt to influence the outcome. In 1986, presidential intervention became even stronger. President Mitterrand had initially aimed for Lionel Jospin, the head of the PS machine, and Laurent Fabius, the head of the ministerial team, to lead the campaign jointly. He believed that Jospin would provide efficient, organisational skills and draw in voters from the left of the political spectrum, while the popular Fabius, with his youthful image, pragmatic views and media skills, would draw in votes from the right and centre. This strategy was undermined, however, by a sudden slump in Fabius' popularity rating after he was bested in a major television debate with Jacques Chirac at the end of October 1985, and by a falling-out between the Prime Minister and the President over Mitterrand's controversial decision to meet the Polish leader General Jaruzelski in December 1985. The President thus decided to enter the campaign fray himself in January 1986 in an attempt to prevent an RPR-UDF landslide.

The President's first campaign interventions were made on television and radio in November and December 1985 and were followed by a powerful New Year's Day address to the French people. Here, he strongly defended his administration's record and stated that the country was now on the right course and that the public should 'not let go of the handrail'. These themes were to be frequently repeated by Mitterrand, Jospin and Fabius in the weeks ahead. The party bullishly argued that France had weathered the 1981-86 recession better than its neighbours and that the government had preserved social unity and order and had made French society more open and equal. They asserted, too, that they had formulated a successful policy blend of socialo-capitalism, combining state intervention and planning, to provide investment funds and training facilities for industrial restructuring and modernisation, while encouraging private initiative and market forces at the factory level. This policy was now, they believed, bearing fruit, with inflation falling to an 18-year low of 3.7%, unemployment displaying a downward trend and real incomes beginning to rise again. The Socialist Party campaign leaders argued, by contrast, that the Right Coalition's tax-cutting, deregulatory policy programme (which they termed *le libéralisme sauvage*) was a dangerous and unjust alternative, which threatened renewed inflation and which, favouring the rich against the poor, risked opening the country to a wave of social disorder of the type which had recently occurred in England's inner cities.

The Socialists thus somewhat curiously, but like previous incumbent administrations, offered the electorate a policy of order and stability and accused the opposition of seeking instability and change. Their campaign was effectively led by President Mitterrand, who, through a skilful blend of impartiality and partisanship, raised his public standing from a level of 40% in November 1985 to one in excess of 50% by February 1986. It involved all the modern American-style razzmatazz which had become common in recent French political campaigns and combined orchestrated public meetings with specially organised television 'events'. The Socialists also made use of their position in government to introduce a number of local vote-influencing initiatives, including the signing of a Channel Tunnel project agreement with the UK government and the sanctioning of £250 million of motorway projects to create jobs in depressed northern France. The Right Coalition leader, Jacques Chirac, also campaigned with typical vigour, as did Jean-Marie Le Pen, but at the local level campaigning was more low-key and mundane, lacking the sharp edge of personality-based contests at the constituency level.

As polling day approached, support for the Socialists began to move up from 25% towards the 30% mark. The party was helped by the release of improved economic statistics and by a squeeze of the PCF vote. Support for the National Front also began to rise, but the RPR and UDF still appeared on course for a parliamentary majority. The Right Coalition's position was strengthened in the final days of the campaign by the government's mishandling of a hostage crisis involving pro-Iranian terrorists based in Beirut, which resulted in the loss of one French hostage's life and a series of bombings in Paris.

The Results of the March 1986 National Assembly Elections

When polling finally took place on Sunday, 16 March, it soon became clear that the President's manoeuvring during the previous year had largely been successful. The Socialists, aided by recent boundary changes by Interior Minister Defferre, emerged as the largest single party in the new Assembly and an RPR-UDF landslide had been averted by the new PR system. The parties of the conventional opposition had to be content instead with the achievement of the barest of parliamentary majorities, 291 seats in a 577-seat Assembly, which was gained on a 44% share of the national vote. (See Table 11.) This promised to leave the President considerable room for manoeuvre during the months ahead.

The performance of the Socialist Party in March 1986 was respectable and heartening for President Mitterrand, recording, with its 31% share of the national vote, its second best ever performance. A number of its disillusioned 1981 supporters decided to abstain, this being reflected in the low turnout of only 78%, but many other more recent supporters remained loyal. The party did particularly well in Lyons (Rhône-Alpes), where its list, led by the popular former Defence Minister Charles Hernu, outpolled Raymond Barre's UDF list by 186 000 votes to 144 000; in Laurent Fabius' Rouen base; and in Paris and Lille, where the PS lists were headed by Lionel Jospin and Pierre Mauroy. Above all, in March 1986 the Socialists clearly established their dominance as the principal party of the Left. The PCF was able to achieve only a desultory 9.8% share of the vote, its worst performance since

TABLE 11 : THE MARCH 1986 NATIONAL ASSEMBLY ELECTIONS (Turnout 78%)

	Votes	% of Total	Assembly Seats[1]
Socialist Party & MRG	8.81m	31.4%	216
Communist Party	2.74m	9.8%	35
Far Left	0.43m	1.5%	—
Other Left	0.34m	1.2%	—
RPR-UDF Combined Lists	6.02m	21.5%	—
RPR Separate List	3.14m	11.2%	148
UDF Separate List	2.33m	8.3%	129
Other Right-wing	1.09m	3.9%	14
National Front	2.71m	9.7%	35
Ecologists	0.34m	1.2%	—

[1] Distributed by party. The RPR-UDF combined list captured 147 seats, the separate RPR list 77 seats and the separate UDF-CDS list 53 seats. Within the Socialist Party-MRG total are included 207 PS seats, 2 MRG seats and 7 *divers gauche* ('various left') seats.

1932 and a figure less than half that which it had regularly achieved before 1981. Its vote collapsed in the Marseilles and Paris regions as well as in the 'couronne' red belt comprising Seine-St Denis, Georges Marchais' Val-de-Marne fiefdom and Hauts-de-Seine, where it captured only six out of 38 seats. PCF support held up, surprisingly, better in rural areas.

The parties of the conventional Right Coalition were, despite gaining an overall majority, disappointed with the result of March 1986. The RPR polled the strongest, although its performance in Chirac's Paris heartland was below par. In particular, it won back much of the 'farm vote', as a result of antipathy to Mitterrand's EEC policies. The UDF polled poorly in Lyons, Rouen, Marseilles and Lille with lists led by Raymond Barre, Jean Lecanuet, Jean-Claude Gaudin and Charles de Gaulle (the former general's grandson). Only Giscard in his Auvergne homeland polled better than expected. Part of the reason for this disappointing performance was a late transfer of centrist support back to the Socialists as a result of President Mitterrand's campaigning efforts. A major factor was also, however, the unexpectedly strong performance of the far-right National Front (FN). The 9.7% of the vote it captured formed a significant portion of the combined Right's 55% share of the national vote. The party polled particularly strongly in Toulon and Marseilles (where it emerged as the second largest party behind the PS) and Lille, gaining a 25% and 20% share of the ballot respectively, and its overall performance compared favourably with the 2.5 million votes captured by the Poujadists in 1956. The FN drew away support from the RPR, UDF and PCF and finished just a fraction behind the Communists in the national total. It entered the National Assembly for the first time and with more than 30 deputies was entitled to form a separate party group.

On 16 March 1986 the first elections for the country's 22 regional assemblies were held at the same time and also under the PR system. In these contests there was a more conclusive victory for the Right Coalition parties, the Socialists, who had previously held the presidency of six regional councils, gaining full control of only two regions: Lille (Nord-Pas-de-Calais) and Limousin. The Right Coalition parties gained direct control, by contrast, of eleven regions, spread across western, central and eastern France, while it indirectly controlled nine other regions, concentrated in southern and northeastern France, with the help of National Front deputies: the latter party gaining, as a result, a number of influential assembly posts, including the vice-presidency of the Languedoc-Rousillon,

Aquitaine, Haute-Normandie, Franche-Comté and Picardie regional councils.

An Assessment of the 1981-1986 'Socialist Experiment'

March 1986, despite Socialist Party relief at its narrow scale of defeat, marked the end of the first quinquennium of rule by a party of the Left since 1799.[1] It was a term of rule which began with great optimism and a flurry of reforms, followed by a period of crisis and confusion, before the government realigned itself and shifted determinedly towards the centre. The party's promise of a thoroughgoing and irreversible transformation of French society remained unfulfilled. Significant changes were, however, effected by the Mitterrand administration between 1981 and 1986 and the landscape of French politics was substantially altered.

The balance sheet of the Mitterrand years was mixed. The Socialist administration failed to adhere to many of its key 1981 campaign promises, for example, the freezing of the nuclear power programme and the ending of state funding to private education. In other areas — the reduction in the working week, the creation of increased civil service employment and the introduction of workers' participation — it made early efforts at reform, before calling a halt as a major U-turn was effected in economic policy from June 1982. In foreign policy and in the style of government, changes were similarly limited.[1] In a number of other areas — nationalisation, the press law and the introduction of PR — reform was substantial but appeared likely to be transient, as the succeeding Right Coalition government set about overturning these measures.

It was in the social and institutional spheres that the Mitterrand administration's achievements were the most appreciable and enduring. It built upon the work commenced during the early Pompidou and Giscard eras and introduced a sweeping range of

[1]   The Left had held power only briefly in the intervening years in 1848, 1870 and 1936.

[1]   In foreign policy, the Mitterrand administration adopted, under the influence of its special adviser Régis Debray, a somewhat more 'South' and Mediterranean orientated approach. In addition, it continued Giscard's moves towards closer European co-operation and the integration of French forces into NATO planning. A broadly Gaullist policy line was still, however, adopted.

reforms aimed at updating the French political and institutional system and creating a more just, open, democratic and united society. Most prominent in this sphere were Justice Minister Robert Badinter and the PCF's Civil Service Minister Anicet Le Pors, who introduced legislation abolishing the death penalty; broadening entry to the prestigious ENA through the reservation of 10 of the 150 annual places for public servants (for example trade unionists) from ordinary backgrounds; and who thoroughly overhauled the judicial and legal system, limiting the previously extensive powers of examining magistrates (*juges d'instruction*) and extending the rights of defendants. Similarly significant social and institutional reforms were effected by the Social Services, Labour and Interior Ministers. These included the extension of workers' bargaining rights; the decentralisation of power-holding and decision-making; the reduction in government control over television and radio stations; the breaching of the airwave monopoly; and the reform of the notoriously regressive French tax system to improve income distribution.

These reforms were of immense importance in furthering the steady transformation of France into a modern, open and pluralistic society on the model of its northern and eastern neighbours, that had been evident during the years since 1968. Thus, while the Mitterrand team failed to effect a lasting and substantial transformation of the French economic system and carry through its threatened 'rupture with capitalism', it did manage to effect most significant and lasting social and political changes. These reforms helped to break the firm 20-year grip of the Right over many of the nation's key institutions and served to create a new, more liberal political culture and a diffused power structure which embraced many previously isolated and excluded groups. The most important such group was the Socialist Party itself, which had at last been given a taste of power. This it exercised with responsibility and judgement, and found itself transformed in the process, abandoning, as Laurent Fabius noted in October 1985, 'the culture of opposition' and embracing 'the culture of government'. The Socialists had established themselves as a substantial and credible centre-left 'social democratic' party of government which was ready to assume power once more in the future when the political pendulum swung back towards the the Left. *Alternance* (alternation) had at last become possible.

Cohabitation: The Mitterrand-Chirac
Government of 1986 —

In March 1986, however, the pendulum of power had swung for the meantime towards the parties of the Right Coalition and France experienced, for the first time during the Fifth Republic, a party political split within its dual executive, as the Socialist President, with two years of his mandate remaining, was now forced to *cohabit* with a Prime Minister and ministerial team drawn from the Right Majority Coalition. The French political system entered uncharted waters and an opportunity was at last provided to test the 1958 constitution and clarify its confused power balance between the Prime Minister and President.

The President could have resigned in March 1986 on losing his parliamentary majority. This is what Raymond Barre and a number of other Right Coalition politicians had called for, viewing the parliamentary election as a quasi-referendum on the Mitterrand presidency. Under the terms of the constitution, however, there was no requirement for such a resignation, and President Mitterrand determined as early as June 1985 that he would remain in office and cohabit with the Right Coalition if the Socialists' Assembly majority was lost. He reconciled himself to the loss of supreme authority over the majority of policy areas, but believed that, in accordance with Article 5 of the constitution, he would be able to retain firm control over defence and foreign policy and would be able, under Article 10, to make his 'reservations' known about aspects of the government's domestic policy with which he disagreed. Mitterrand hoped, in such a manner, not to become a bypassed, 'lame duck' figurehead but to retain a high public profile as an active statesman on the international scene. He would leave the new Right Coalition government to deal with the trickier and more intractable problems of domestic policy, intermittently interjecting his own criticisms at judicious intervals. Through such a strategy the President sought to wean support back towards the Socialist Party in readiness for a triumphant election campaign in 1988.

The slenderness of the Right Coalition's majority in March 1986 and the support given in public opinion polls to the idea of cohabitation were two final factors which persuaded President Mitterrand to remain in office after the National Assembly elections. On television on the evening of Monday, 17 March he acknowledged the new majority, wished it well and declared that

105

the new Prime Minister would be drawn from its ranks. A number of political commentators suggested that he might look beyond the ranks of the recognised leaders of the Right Coalition and choose a moderate as a 'consensus Prime Minister', for example Jacques Chaban-Delmas (70), an old Resistance colleague and friend of the President, or Simone Veil. Mitterrand decided, however, to respect the balance of party forces in the new National Assembly and invited Jacques Chirac, leader of the largest party within the majority coalition, to form a new government. The two discussed terms and conditions on 18 March and Chirac, after consulting with Right Coalition colleagues, formally accepted the President's offer of prime ministerial office on 20 March.

It rapidly became clear, however, that the new Prime Minister had different views on the interpretation of the 1958 constitution and on the division of executive responsibilities. Chirac, pointing to Article 20 which granted the Prime Minister and his ministerial team the broad authority to 'determine and direct the policy of the nation', accepted office only on the condition that the President agreed not deliberately to frustrate the implementation of the new government's election programme. Chirac, secondly, was determined that the President should not expropriate foreign and defence policy, with all its *gloire* and glamour, as a special 'presidential preserve', leaving him to concentrate on mundane domestic affairs. He argued convincingly that many foreign policy issues, for example EEC policy, defence spending and participation in the American 'Star Wars' programme, had economic repercussions which the government should consider in full and that, in any case, the Prime Minister was given a clear responsibility for national defence under Article 21 of the constitution and that his countersignature was required for treaty ratification. Chirac thus called for a co-operative and joint approach to foreign affairs, but in other policy areas saw the Prime Minister as the dominant partner, with the President remaining in the background as an aloof arbiter.

President Mitterrand conceded a number of these points during his 18 March meeting with Chirac in return for the right to have an influence over the composition of the Prime Minister's new cabinet. Such early, mutual displays of flexibility improved the prospects of success for the cohabitation experiment. Significant differences still existed, however, between the two men's perception of their roles, personalities and policy outlook. The President viewed Chirac as an impetuous and overly ambitious figure and firmly opposed a number of his domestic policy proposals. The Prime Minister was, for his part, suspicious of the President, who, nicknamed 'Florentine' as a result of his reputation for scheming Machiavellianism, appeared likely to lay traps to embarrass and ensnare Chirac in the months ahead.

Major executive conflicts thus appeared likely over foreign affairs, interference in which President Mitterrand said he would view as amounting to a *coup d'état*, and at home over denationalisation. The Prime Minister would need, however, to worry not just about the President's views and actions, but also those of the Constitutional Council, following the election of new members in 1983 and 1986, and his Right Coalition partners. The Constitutional Council now boasted a narrow Socialist majority, having as its chairman since February 1986, the former Justice Minister, Robert Badinter. It would act as the constitutional referee in disputes between Mitterrand and Chirac and would carefully scrutinise the legality of the government's new legislative proposals. An even greater threat, however, to the Chirac government was that of parliamentary revolt. On paper the Right Coalition's majority, dependent on the support of 14 *divers droite* deputies, was wafer-thin and could rapidly be eroded by new by-elections. Within this majority there was, in addition, an assemblage of groups with different policy outlooks. In many votes the Right Coalition could look forward to seeing its majority boosted by the support of outcast National Front deputies. On contentious issues, however, there was a strong threat of revolt from within UDF ranks and particularly from the 14 'right-wing independents' within the coalition: the two most prominent of these independents were Marie-France Garaud, a maverick Gaullist, and Dominique Baudis, the mayor of Toulouse.[1]

Cohabitation in Practice: the Chirac Government's Early Record

Prime Minister Chirac's first days in office were preoccupied with the assembly of new private and ministerial cabinet teams. His choice of the ministerial cabinet was influenced by discussions with fellow leaders within the RPR and UDF, but its final composition (see Table 12) proved to be strongly Chiraquian in mould. Of its members 20 were drawn from the RPR, compared to only

---

[1] Raymond Barre and his group of 26 UDF deputies pledged, despite their opposition to *cohabitation*, not to bring the new government down.

TABLE 12 : LEADING POSTS IN THE CHIRAC CABINET OF MARCH 1986[1]

Prime Minister	J Chirac (53) RPR
Economy, Finance & Privatisation	E Balladur (56) RPR
Interior	C Pasqua (58) RPR
Justice	A Chalandon (65) RPR
Foreign Affairs	J-B Raimond (60) NP
Defence	A Giraud (62) NP
Social Affairs & Labour	P Séguin (42) RPR
Education	R Monory (62) UDF
Culture & Communications	F Léotard (43) UDF
Equipment, Housing & Transport	P Mehaignerie (46) UDF
Agriculture	F Guillaume (54) RPR
Co-operation	M Aurillac (57) RPR
Parliament Relations	A Rossinot (46) UDF
Industry, Posts & Tourism	A Madelin (37) UDF
Overseas Departments & Territories	B Pons (59) RPR

[1]   NP refers to non-party. Eight other ministers sat in the cabinet, while there were 15 additional junior ministers. This government team, including only three women (all junior ministers), was far more male-dominated than the Mitterrand or Giscard teams, which had included six and five women respectively.

---

seventeen from the UDF, with the UDF receiving the less important posts of culture, education and housing while the key domestic portfolios were monopolised by close RPR colleagues of the Prime Minister. The pre-eminent concerns of the new administration would be the economy and crime, thus the significant appointments were the troika of Édouard Balladur (Economy and Finance), Philippe Séguin (Social Affairs) and Charles Pasqua (Interior Ministry). Balladur, a Turkish-born énarque, was a committed advocate of the new free-market *libéralisme* and had served successively as secretary-general in the Pompidou 'cabinet' of 1973/4 and as a political adviser to Jacques Chirac. Séguin, a *pied noir*, Tunisian-born *énarque* and mayor of Épinal, had also previously served as an adviser to Chirac's protégé, Georges Pompidou. Pasqua, the Corsican-born, former RPR Senate leader from the Midi region, was once connected with the banned rightist SAC militia and had strong views on combating crime and dealing with the immigrant issue. A fourth significant Chiraquian appointment to the new cabinet was François Guillaume, president of the right-wing FNSEA (*Fédération Nationale des Syndicats des Exploitants Agricoles*) Farmers' Union, who was given the Agriculture portfolio and would pursue policies favouring the farm lobby.

Such appointments, however, while serving to establish Jacques Chirac's dominance over the domestic policy of the new government, promised to exacerbate tensions and divisions within the Right Coalition. The UDF was, not surprisingly, bitterly disappointed with the scale and significance of its representation in the new cabinet. Some of its younger leaders, for example François Léotard (secretary-general of the RP) and Pierre Mehaignerie (president of the CDS), had been given important portfolios; its more senior leaders, however, found themselves excluded. The UDF president, Jean Lecanuet (66), was originally proposed as Foreign Minister, but his appointment was rejected by President Mitterrand, who sought to exclude 'heavyweight' politicians from what he saw as his own sphere of interest. A career diplomat, Jean-Bernard Raimond, was thus selected for the *Quai d'Orsay* instead, while André Giraud, an engineer technocrat who had served as Industry Minister between 1978-81, was selected for the Defence Ministry, after President Mitterrand had vetoed the appointment of François Léotard to this post. The other important UDF leader who had looked forward to a return to high office in March 1986 was the former President, Valéry Giscard d'Estaing. He set his sights on returning to the Finance Ministry, thus gaining an influence over economic policy, but this was rejected by Jacques Chirac, who preferred to have his 'own man' installed in this key post. As an alternative, Giscard would have been satisfied with being elected into the prestigious post of president of the National Assembly, which would have given him an influence over the arrangement of parliamentary business and appointments to the Constitutional Council. Again, however, Chirac failed to give his support to the former President, and the post went instead to Jacques Chaban-Delmas of the RPR. Chirac thus managed rapidly to antagonise the key elder statesmen within the UDF and would need to be on his guard against parliamentary revolt during the months ahead. He had also, by opting for a narrow ideological base to his cabinet, linked his own personal reputation and future prospects closely to the policy fortunes of the new government.

The policy programme of the new Chirac government had been set out clearly in the January 1986 RPR-UDF 'joint manifesto'. There were sufficient similarities between this manifesto and the Fabius administration's 1984-86 approach to foreign and domestic affairs to suggest that cohabitation might prove feasible. The underlying philosophies behind the Fabius-Mitterand and Chirac programmes remained, however, substantially different, emanating, as the President noted, from 'two different systems of thought', socialism and conservative liberalism, with diverging goals and interpretations of human behaviour. These differences were particularly visible in the economic sphere, where the Chirac administration was anxious to travel far further down the deregulatory, free-market road than the Fabius team had ever contemplated, and in the approach to criminal affairs and civil rights.

Jacques Chirac set out three sets of policy priorities at the outset of his administration: economic restructuring to create the conditions for renewed growth; a tough new anti-crime and anti-terrorism campaign; and repeal of PR and the reintroduction of the first-past-the-post two-ballot electoral system. He was anxious to implement these changes rapidly during a whirlwind first hundred days in office in which he would 'liberalise' and 'desocialise' France's economy and institutions, repealing a number of the key reforms of 1981-86, and to establish his own imprint on the French polity in time for new elections which the President might be tempted to call at any moment. To carry out key elements of this programme at speed, for example privatisation and electoral reform, he gained permission from the President to present enabling legislation to parliament to allow him to rule in specific areas by ordinance.

Economic reform was the centrepiece of the Chirac policy programme, with the new government seeking radically to roll back the frontiers of state interference and promising to lift price and exchange controls, free the housing and labour markets, markedly reduce taxation and public spending, squeeze state industrial aid and denationalise a major portion of the public sector. The Prime Minister and his Economy and Finance Minister Édouard Balladur set about this task with relish in March 1986, but also displayed a shrewd mixture of pragmatic caution, aware that over-zealous implementation of the new deregulatory programme would, in the short term, serve dangerously to fuel inflation and unemployment. They eased price and exchange controls in two stages in April and

May 1986, and, a month later, abolished the Socialists' 1982 Rent Act, removed the 20-year-old restriction on firms being able to dismiss employees without prior government agreement and introduced a 'supplementary budget' which abolished the wealth tax and reduced the tax burden on industry. These measures were forced through parliament against fierce Socialist and PCF opposition, but, with the support of National Front deputies, were carried with majorities of more than 30. They formed part of a 'supply side' approach, aimed at rendering French industry more flexible and internationally competitive, which was implemented within the broader framework of tight monetary and public spending control. This policy approach was complemented by a number of specific measures aimed at boosting growth and employment, for example currency devaluation in April 1986 and the introduction of a 'new frontier' job subsidisation programme for workers under the age of 25.

The most central and controversial element in the Chirac administration's 'new economic programme' was, however, its plan to privatise 65 state-owned companies and banks employing 800 000 people. This privatisation programme was aimed at radically redrawing the balance between state and private enterprise in France, freeing companies from government interference and providing the government with 'windfall revenue' from asset sales expected to average FFr 60 billion per annum. It involved the sale of state banking and insurance companies, the TF-1 television network and the industrial giants which had been nationalised by the Socialists in 1982. The pace of denationalisation was largely to be determined by stock market considerations, with enabling legislation being passed as early as the middle of May 1986. President Mitterrand was, however, strongly opposed to many of these proposed sales and stated as early as April 1986 that he would refuse to sign decrees privatising banks which had been taken over by the de Gaulle government of 1944-46. He carried out this threat on 14 July, Bastille Day, stating that the terms of the decree for privatising 65 state companies failed to include sufficient safeguards to ensure that a proper price was paid and that the 'national heritage' did not fall into foreign hands.[1] The President's actions failed, however, to disrupt the privatisation schedule.

[1] Under the 1958 constitution the President was obliged to sign bills passed by parliament within 15 days. There was no such obligation for decrees, which needed the countersignature of the President.

Chirac instead rushed the bill through the National Assembly, successfully imposing a 'guillotine' on 24 July, and had, by mid August, replaced the heads of half of the firms earmarked for privatisation in preparation for flotation in the autumn.[1]

The Chirac administration's efforts in the sphere of law and order during its first 100 days in office were even more striking, as it sought to make an immediate impression on voters who, worried by the rising crime rate, had deserted the RPR and voted for the National Front in March 1986. The forceful new Interior Minister, Charles Pasqua, whose appointment President Mitterrand had sought, but failed, to veto, and the Security and Justice Ministers, Robert Pandraud and Albin Chalandon, were anxious to increase the resources given to the police, extend their powers for combating crime and raise penal sentences as a means of deterrence.[2] In their first goal, they differed little from the previous Socialist administration, whose Interior Minister, Pierre Joxe, had launched a major police recruitment and modernisation campaign in 1985. In their second goal, however, the differences were stark, as the extension of police powers began to infringe upon civil liberties. Computerised identity cards were introduced, the controls against illegal immigration severely tightened and new powers for random identity checks were now granted to the police. The new government also made a concerted effort to combat the growing menace of domestic and international terrorism.[3] A new terrorist code was promulgated, cross-border police co-operation improved and a special co-ordinating Security Council, under the chairmanship of the Prime Minister and including the Interior, Defence, Justice, Foreign and Defence Ministers, was established.

---

[1] The first companies to be successfully privatised were the Saint-Gobain glass giant (December 1986) and the Paribas finance company (January 1987), with the Assurances Générales de France finance house set to follow in the spring of 1987.

[2] The sentence for capital offences was increased, for example, from 18 years to a non-commutable 30 years, although the death penalty was not restored.

[3] Domestic terrorist groups, for example the ultra-leftist *Action Directe* and Middle East based Islamic groups, had become increasingly involved in bombing incidents on French soil between 1985/6. These outrages peaked in September 1986 with six bomb explosions in the space of thirteen days, resulting in the loss of twelve lives and injuries to 170, as efforts were made to force the release of Georges Ibrahim Abdallah, the imprisoned leader of the Lebanese Armed Revolutionary Factions (FARL).

The third element of the new administration's policy programme, the return to the first-past-the-post electoral system, was of vital and urgent political importance for Prime Minister Chirac.[1] Its implementation, which, combined with boundary redrawing, was seen to be worth at least 60 seats to the RPR-UDF alliance, would almost certainly guarantee that the ruling coalition would maintain its parliamentary majority in new elections, thus removing the threat of a sudden dissolution of the National Assembly by President Mitterrand. Such a reform change was, however, strongly, and not surprisingly, opposed by the National Front and PCF minor parties, as well as by the Socialists and a number of UDF 'independents'. It was not certain of passage in an ordinary parliamentary vote. Prime Minister Chirac therefore decided to rush the reform through by decree, forcing through the enabling bill by 'guillotine' on 20 May. He was successful in this endeavour but his actions proved to be controversial and damaging, being viewed as a grave affront to democratic debate by an opposition whose vote of censure failed by only five votes on 23 May.

Prime Minister Chirac concentrated his attention during his first three months in office on domestic affairs, thus giving tacit recognition to President Mitterrand's claim for supremacy over foreign affairs. Chirac did not, however, fully renounce his interest in the latter sector. He maintained a powerful and experienced seven-member foreign policy advisory team at the Hôtel Matignon under the leadership of the former diplomat François Bujon de l'Estaing, which included the old Gaullist African expert Jacques Foccart (73), and he insisted on meeting visitors to France and attending overseas summits, for example the May 1986 'world economic summit' in Tokyo. Prime Minister Chirac also intervened in foreign affairs periodically with minor initiatives of his own, the four most important being: the decision to pull out part of the French observer force from Beirut in April 1986; the alteration of the New Caledonia bill in June 1986 (withdrawing the autonomy that Mitterrand had sought to grant to the new Kanak-dominated regional councils); a call for French participation in SDI research; and the negotiated release from New Zealand in July 1986 of the two secret service agents involved in the Rainbow Warrior mining. In many areas there was a broad accordance of views between the

---

[1] The Chirac reform change entailed maintenance of the present number of 577 Assembly seats.

President and Prime Minister, but over New Caledonia and SDI the divergence was substantial, resulting in a significant rightward shift in France's foreign policy approach.

An Assessment of Cohabitation and Chirac's Early Record

The Fifth Republic's first experiment in power-sharing between President and Prime Minister proved to be a most awkward and delicate affair for both participants. Each was anxious to, at least initially, make the new cohabitation system work, particularly Jacques Chirac, who was aware that failure would strengthen support for Raymond Barre. Each was also, however, keen to emerge as the dominant 'victor' in the new power structure. The months after March 1986 were characterised by complex and skilful jockeying and manoeuvring by two flexible and experienced politicians in what was described as a 'reverse western' in which the first man to draw risked getting himself killed.

The first two months of the cohabitation experiment were a honeymoon period in which both men pragmatically gave ground over contentious issues and displayed studied politeness in their mutual relations. The public responded warmly to this approach and gave 70% support for the new 'balanced' system of government and 50% approval ratings for both Mitterrand and Chirac. Slowly but surely, however, it was President Mitterrand who began to emerge as the real victor from cohabitation. In terms of power wielded, he became clearly subordinate to the new Prime Minister, the President seeing only the late drafts of government bills and presiding in a largely formal manner over the weekly Council of Ministers' meetings. However, the President made clear his 'reservations' about many of the Chirac administration's domestic measures, setting himself up as the defender of the 'national interest' and the 'national heritage' of popular social legislation. He laid down policy 'markers' and intervened forcefully on occasion, refusing, for example, to sign proposed decrees on the removal of labour protection and on denationalisation in April and July 1986. The President also played an active role on the international scene, visiting Washington and Moscow in July 1986, to maintain a high and statesmanlike public profile.

This 'arbiter strategy' began to pay dividends for President Mitterrand by the early summer of 1986, his opinion poll rating rising to a record 62% in mid July. Prime Minister Chirac's popularity rating slumped by contrast to only 48%, as the public became concerned with his high-handed approach to parliament, seen in the frequent use of decrees and the 'guillotine', with his failure to stem the rising tide of unemployment and with his partisanship on many issues. Two examples of the latter were the economic measures he introduced between March and August 1986, which favoured businesses and farming groups at the expense of public sector workers, and the decision to privatise the popular TV-1 network and resell Channels 5 and 6, largely as a result of their alleged left-wing bias.[1]

This growing opposition from the Centre and Left significantly increased during the closing months of 1986 as controversial social reform packages were unveiled by the new administration. In November 1986 Justice Minister Albin Chalandon proposed more rigorous restrictions for the acquisition of French citizenship[2] and unveiled plans to privatise elements of the prison service. In the same month, Alain Devaquet (RPR), the minister for higher education, introduced into the National Assembly an education bill designed to make entry into universities more selective and expensive. This measure provoked a wave of spontaneous student demonstrations in November-December 1986 which turned violent in Paris following the death of a student of Algerian descent on 6 December at the hands of the CRS riot police. The level of student protest, more than half a million marching through Paris during a national day of protest on 4 December, surprised and unnerved the Chirac administration and created tensions between the Prime Minister and UDF cabinet members, most notably François Léotard and Alain Madelin, who were fiercely critical of the Devaquet reform measure. With public support and sympathy for the students mounting, Alain Devaquet tendered his resignation and the *Loi Devaquet* (higher education bill) was withdrawn from the National Assembly by Jacques Chirac on 8 December. A day later, Prime Minister Chirac also announced that a special session of parliament would not be called in January 1987, thus postponing introduction of the equally controversial Chalandon nationality

---

[1]   Conservative consortia, including one led by Robert Hersant, seemed likely to acquire the new franchises.

[2]   The 'Chalandon reforms' sought in future to subject anyone born of non-French parents on French soil to an 18-month probationary period, with citizenship in future to be refused to anyone with a criminal record or who was unable to speak French according to his or her 'social level'.

and prison privatisation bills.[1] This represented a humiliating defeat for Prime Minister Chirac and served to increase support for President Mitterrand, who had made clear his opposition to the *Loi Devaquet* at an early date and who had played a key role in forcing the bill's withdrawal.

Within days of the conclusion of the campus crisis, Prime Minister Chirac encountered a second and potentially more serious challenge to his authority from public sector workers, following a chain of events which recalled in many respects the 'May events' of 1968. During the years of Socialist rule between 1981 and 1986, France's notoriously active trade union movement had been relatively docile and its leadership had in large measure co-operated with government-imposed wage-freeze programmes. Matters changed with the election to power of the Chirac administration, which sought, as part of its broader anti-inflation programme, to restrict wage increases in the public sector to only 2-3% per annum while at the same time introducing substantial tax concessions for the better-off. In addition, the new government failed regularly to consult trade union leaders and, with its policy of easing the restrictions on the dismissal of workers, was viewed as a close ally of the *patronat*. An early indication of the changing attitude of trade unionists was to be found in the widespread support given by public sector workers to the call for a one-day national strike on 21 October 1986. It was, however, workers on the SNCF (*Société Nationale des Chemins de Fer Français*) state railway network who lit the fuse which ignited a serious 'winter of discontent' by walking out from work on 18 December 1986 in opposition both to the public sector pay ceiling and to a more specific attempt by the Chirac administration to replace the SNCF's traditional seniority pay grade system with new merit-based salary scales. Rank-and-file members took the lead in a strike which began at the Paris Gare du Nord, spread to the south and rapidly gained national support, paralysing the SNCF network at a cost to the nation of £9 million a day. This rail strike became the longest experienced in post-war France, lasting for 26 days, and it encouraged similar action by seamen, electricity industry workers, postmen and Paris bus and metro employees, who walked out from

[1] On 16 January 1987 Justice Minister Chalandon announced that the introduction of the 'Nationality Bill' would be shelved pending broader discussion with human rights organisations, church leaders and opposition parties. This rendered introduction of the measure unlikely before the 1988 presidential election.

work during January 1987, bringing, as a consequence, large-scale power cuts and a sharp fall in the value of the French Franc. Prime Minister Chirac, recognising the gravity of the crisis, cancelled his proposed winter break in Tunisia to take charge of the crisis. He was forced, however, to make concessions to the workers, including withdrawal of the proposed SNCF merit pay scheme and the sanction of a number of breaches of the 3% public sector pay increase ceiling, before succeeding in effecting a general return to work during the middle of January 1987. Chirac was aided in this process by the actions of the communist CGT, which tried to transform the sporadic strike activity into a politicised movement against the government in a manner which alienated rank-and-file workers.

Prime Minister Chirac weathered the industrial storm of December 1986 — January 1987 which served to polarise opinion in the nation. As the weather grew colder in January 1987, public sympathy for the public sector strikers diminished. It was less the Prime Minister, however, but more President Mitterrand, who, like de Gaulle in 1968, was to benefit from a rallying of support around the government at a time of national crisis. Mitterrand, continuing to project himself skilfully as an 'above-party' conciliatory and monarchical figure, received a deputation of three striking railway workers at the height of the crisis and urged the preservation of national unity. In addition, he continued to make plain his opposition to controversial government reforms, refusing to sign for example the new employment law decree (easing the restrictions on hiring and firing and on hours of labour) in October 1986. Through such actions President Mitterrand gained a clear lead of more than ten points (40% to 50%) over Prime Minister Chirac in opinion polls conducted during the spring of 1987. Drawing sustenance from this continuing high level of popular support, the President became more assertive in his dealings with Prime Minister Chirac in what became termed a new phase of *cohabitension*. President Mitterrand appeared to be well positioned to emerge victorious from any leadership conflict between the Élysée Palace and Hôtel Matignon. His prospects of re-election in May 1988 or at an earlier date, if tempted to call a referendum on a shortening of the presidential term to five years and put himself forward for immediate re-election, had also significantly improved since the nadir of 1983/4.

Presidential and Party Prospects for 1988?

The most striking aspect of the *cohabitation experiment* has been the manner in which the French political system has been radically reforged in a calm and mature fashion, with presidential supremacy giving way to prime ministerial pre-eminence and Assembly deputies recapturing the power to make and break the incumbent government. This change may be the precursor to a more fundamental restructuring of the French political system on either the American separation of powers model or on the British-German parliamentary model. It may, however, be only a temporary split-executive dilemma. Which direction the French constitution takes will very largely depend upon the outcome of the next presidential and parliamentary elections.

At present the French political scene is divided between the Socialist Party, presenting a moderate, centre-left, 'social democratic' policy programme, and the RPR-UDF coalition, grouped around a new, free-market, liberal approach to economic affairs.[1] These two groupings monopolise more than 80% of public support, with the predominant share being held by the RPR-UDF. The policy differences between the two groupings remain substantial on economic and social affairs, but have narrowed significantly during the last decade. On either wing of these groupings are two small extremist parties, the National Front and PCF, each attracting almost 10% of the national vote. One of these, the National Front, is a 'flash party' whose future prospects are most uncertain. The other, the PCF, appears to be in a state of terminal decline with its membership aging and thinning. There were growing calls in the months after March 1986 for internal party reform and democratisation and for the replacement of Georges Marchais (65) as general-secretary by a unifying figure such as Charles Fiterman.[2] Even with such a 'renovation', however, the party will find it difficult to draw back lost voters in the years ahead

---

[1] The Socialist Party's shift to the centre gained further momentum in April 1986 when Jean-Pierre Chevènement's CERES faction was disbanded and renamed the 'Socialism and Republic' group, dropping its adherence to Marxist doctrines, for example class struggle and the 'break with capitalism', and ending its support for alliance with the PCF.

[2] At the PCF's Central Committee meeting of January 1987 unprecedented divisions emerged in the party, with Politburo member Claude Poperen resigning along with Central Committee member Marcel Rigout.

and seems destined to become a rump party, retaining control of a diminishing number of local strongholds in the traditional 'red belt' zone of northern France.

French politics appears to be taking on a two-party hue, which remains, however, complicated by the presidential system. In parliamentary elections the RPR-UDF coalition seems destined to hold the upper hand, having held control of the National Assembly for all but five years of the Fifth Republic. In presidential elections, however, strong divisions have increasingly emerged between leaders within the Right Coalition. This opened the door for François Mitterrand in 1981 and may do so again in 1987 or 1988. President Mitterrand, who will be 71 in 1988 and who has already (in 1977 and 1981) undergone minor cancer treatment, has suggested on a number of occasions since March 1986 that he may not stand again for a further seven-year term. In the absence of Mitterrand the Socialist Party would appear to be threatened with dissension between the rival candidacies of Michel Rocard, Laurent Fabius and Lionel Jospin. At a special meeting of the PS executive meeting in February 1987, however, Michel Rocard agreed not to run against Mitterrand if the President did decide to run again and all intra-party factions consented to a joint motion that the PS candidate for 1988 should be chosen 'at the appropriate time' and should receive 'undivided support'. In the Right Coalition, by contrast, intense feuding continues between the 'party barons'. Valéry Giscard d'Estaing, influenced by the continuing decline in his national support, announced in a peak-time television address in February 1987 that he would not contest the 1988 presidential election, although he did add, 'should our country be faced in the future with grave problems, you will always be able to count on me'. Prime Minister Chirac will still face, however, fierce opposition from Giscard's protégé, the young liberal RP leader François Léotard (44), and particularly from former Prime Minister Raymond Barre. Barre, having opposed the cohabitation experiment from the outset, appeared, among Right Coalition supporters, justified in his views following the events of November 1986 — January 1987. The principled and sententious Barre recovered from a sharp slump in his national standing during the March 1986 National Assembly elections to emerge as the single most popular politician in the country in opinion polls taken during the spring of 1987, enjoying an approval rating of 55%. Chirac's record in office since March 1986, involving the alternation of impetuosity and authoritarianism with hesitancy and capitulation and his reopening of many of the country's traditional social divisions, has, by contrast, seriously damaged his prospects of gaining the 1988 presidential nomination for the Right Coalition. However, whichever candidate emerges dominant following the first ballot in 1988, an alienation of supporters from the opposing UDF and RPR wings appears likely on the subsequent second ballot of the presidential contest, dividing the Right Coalition vote to the Socialist candidate's advantage.[1] A Socialist Party victory in subsequent snap Assembly elections would appear, however, for the reasons noted in the concluding section, to be more problematical. Failure to achieve such a victory would add momentum to the calls for thoroughgoing constitutional reform.

A Rightward Shift in French Political Culture?

Although the Socialists may hope, as a result of divisions within the Right Coalition, to retain the presidency in 1988, ideologically and in party terms the later 1980s, as a consequence of secular economic and social changes, promises to be a period dominated by the Right.

During the 1960s and 1970s, rapid industrialisation and urbanisation (see pages 16 and 24) provided an expanding bedrock of support for the parties of the Left, particularly the PS, which became the party most reflective of contemporary society, *le parti de temps*. Since 1981, however, the Left's support base has been significantly eroded by an economic recession, out of which France is only just emerging (see Appendix A Table 1), which struck most severely the older industrialised regions of Socialist-PCF-dominated north-eastern France. In Nord-Pas-de-Calais and Lorraine, the troubled 'smokestack' coal, steel, shipbuilding and textile industries were decimated by the slump in European demand and by a sharpening in competition from overseas NICs. In the Paris region, the automobile industry, the great success story of post-war France, was also seriously affected by the shift to new automated technology and by growing overproduction within the European car market. Taken together, the proportion of the French workforce employed in the manufacturing sector declined sharply

---

[1] Chirac has, in addition, alienated the potential 'second ballot' support from National Front voters as a result of the May 1986 abolition of PR which led Jean-Marie Le Pen to declare his determination to withhold future backing of the RPR.

from 39% in 1975 to barely 30% in 1984, with further reductions of more than 20% in total manufacturing employment being projected for between 1984-88. By contrast, these years were ones of relative growth for the previously under-industrialised regions of western and southern France, for example Bretagne, Aquitaine, Provence-Côte-d'Azur, Midi-Pyrénées and Languedoc-Roussillon. Drawing upon the attractions of their climate and local environment and helped by the planning efforts of DATAR, these regions emerged as centres for new industries — a high-tech 'Silicon Corridor' emerging between Bordeaux, Toulouse and Marseilles — attracting young technicians and professionals from the cities of the north as well as providing employment for children from declining local small farming families. Appendix A Table 2 sets out the most recent of these regional economic trends. Recent years have also witnessed a revival in the small firms sector, a general movement away from cities and towards rural commuter villages and, most importantly a major structural shift in the overall pattern of employment towards the service sector, in which the numbers employed rose from 51% of the total workforce in 1975 to 61% in 1984.

These regional and occupational trends, coupled with the progressive aging of the nation's population — a consequence of the delayed effects of the decline in the French birthrate since the 1960s — and increased affluence among the employed, have strengthened the support base of the parties of the Right Coalition and have had a perceptible impact upon popular mentalities, fostering a more individualist and pragmatic approach to political issues. They have been disastrous for the doctrinaire, blue-collar-based PCF. The Socialist Party, however, which has always polled well among white-collar service groups, has adapted to the changed circumstances of 1980s France, pragmatically swinging towards the right in ideological outlook and seeking out new bases of support in fast-developing western and southern France. Above all, however, the consequence of recent economic and social changes has been to weaken popular loyalties for individual parties and to create a more fluid, fickle and unpredictable political landscape. In addition, they have served to bring to an end the traditional 'Loire valley' divide in French political loyalties between Left and Right and to create instead a more uniformly national spread of support for the RPR-UDF and PS, as the March National Assembly and Regional Council elections graphically demonstrated.

FRENCH ECONOMIC INDICATORS, 1977-1986

	Industrial Growth	Wages	Prices	Money Supply Growth	$ Trade Balance	Jobless Rate	FFr per $ Exchange Rate
1977	+ 2.0%	+ 13%	+ 9%	+ 8%	− 3500m	5.6%	4.8
1978	+ 1.5%	+ 13%	+ 9%	+ 10%	+ 900m	6.1%	4.2
1979	+ 4.0%	+ 12%	+ 11%	+ 12%	− 2300m	6.7%	4.1
1980	− 6.0%	+ 16%	+ 13%	+ 9%	− 12700m	7.1%	4.5
1981	− 1.5%	+ 14%	+ 14%	+ 13%	− 10400m	8.9%	5.7
1982	− 4.0%	+ 16%	+ 9%	+ 14%	− 14200m	9.6%	6.9
1983	+ 2.3%	+ 10%	+ 10%	+ 11%	− 7900m	9.5%	8.6
1984	+ 1.6%	+ 8%	+ 7%	+ 2%	− 2900m	10.8%	9.5
1985	+ 0.0%	+ 6%	+ 5%	+ 7%	− 2700m	10.7%	7.7
1986	+ 2.2%	+ 4%	+ 2%	+ 5%	− 1200m	10.6%	6.4

APPENDIX A : TABLE 2

REGIONAL ECONOMIC AND SOCIAL INDICATORS

	AREA (Sq Km)	1982 POPU-LATION	1975-82 POPU-LATION CHANGE	1984 JOBLESS RATE	CHIEF TOWN
NORTH-EASTERN					
Alsace	8280	1 566 048	+ 2.3%	7.0%	Strasbourg
Champagne-Ardenne	25 606	1 345 935	− 0.7%	9.8%	Reims
Lorraine	23 547	2 319 905	− 2.5%	9.6%	Nancy
Nord-Pas-de-Calais	12 414	3 932 939	− 0.3%	12.2%	Lille
Franche-Comté	16 202	1 084 049	− 1.6%	8.4%	Besançon
NORTHERN					
Haute-Normandie	12 317	1 655 362	+ 0.1%	11.6%	Rouen
Île de France	12 012	10 073 059	+ 1.4%	7.4%	Paris
Picardie	19 399	1 740 321	+ 2.5%	10.3%	Amiens
WEST-N.WESTERN					
Basse-Normandie	17 589	1 350 979	+ 2.5%	10.3%	Caen
Bretagne	27 208	2 707 886	+ 2.7%	10.3%	Rennes
Pays de la Loire	32 082	2 930 398	+ 4.1%	10.5%	Nantes
Poitou-Charentes	25 810	1 568 230	+ 0.5%	10.7%	Poitiers
CENTRAL					
Auvergne	26 013	1 332 678	+ 1.4%	8.9%	Clermont-Ferrand
Bourgogne	31 582	1 596 054	+ 0.6%	9.2%	Dijon
Centre	39 151	2 264 164	+ 4.9%	8.2%	Orléans
Limousin	16 942	737 153	+ 2.1%	7.4%	Limoges
SOUTH-WESTERN					
Aquitaine	41 308	2 656 544	+ 3.6%	10.7%	Bordeaux
Midi-Pyrénées	45 348	2 325 319	+ 1.5%	9.4%	Toulouse
SOUTH-EASTERN					
Languedoc-Roussillon	27 376	1 926 514	+ 6.5%	13.2%	Montpellier
Provence-Côte d'Azur	31 400	3 965 209	+ 6.9%	11.7%	Marseilles
Rhône-Alpes	43 698	5 015 947	+ 3.0%	7.8%	Lyon
Corsica	8680	240 178	− 4.5%	11.8%	Ajaccio
ALL FRANCE	543 965	54 334 871	+ 3.2%	10.6%	Paris

THE FRENCH TRADE UNION MOVEMENT, 1974 — 1987

The organisation of the French labour movement has traditionally been intermediate between the British and West German models. In Britain, trade unions have been organised on a craft basis which has resulted in a multiplicity of medium-sized unions — more than 100 existing in 1981 — rendering control by a central organisation, the TUC (Trades Union Congress) largely ineffective. In West Germany, trade unions have been organised on a broader factory and regional basis. Seventeen major unions exist, with one organisation, IG Metall, accounting for a third of total West German labour organisation membership. The central trades union council, the DGB (*Deutscher Gewerkschaftsbund*) has been able to co-ordinate actions in a successful manner and enter into a regular corporatist dialogue with German industrialists and the incumbent government. In France, elements of both the British and West German systems exist. For example, French union organisations, as in Britain, cross industrial boundaries, rendering pay bargaining a chaotic and protracted business. As in West Germany, however, French unions are also grouped into a small number of broader confederations. The distinguishing features of the French labour movement, in contrast to both the British and West German, however, have been its notorious weakness in numerical, political and financial terms, its sharp internal divisions and its militancy and volatility. A number of these features have grown more pronounced during recent years.

The French trade union movement has centred around six confederate organisations, the CGT, CFDT, FO, CFTC, CGC and CSL which, as a result of traditional religious, regional and ideological cleavages, have been mutually antagonistic. The *CGT (Conférédation Générale du Travail)*, founded in 1895, has long been the single most powerful union body, enjoying a long-standing base in the steel, coal, construction, automobile, chemical and electricity industries and in rail and sea transport. Intimately linked with the PCF, its general-secretary (since June 1982 Henri Krasucki) being drawn from the Communist Party's Politburo, it has repeatedly sought to politicise labour disputes, calling frequent 'days of action' against incumbent governments. During elections to labour tribunal boards (which are established to settle work disputes) in 1979 and 1982, the CGT's 40% share of the vote clearly indicated its dominant standing. The second most powerful confederation (enjoying a 24% share of labour board votes in 1979 and 1982) and the principal union force in the private sector, has been the *CFDT (Confédération Française Démocratique du Travail)*. Established in 1919 and led since 1971 by Edmond Maire, the CFDT, although not directly linked to the PS, has been Socialist in sympathy and has been a firm proponent of *autogestion* (workers' control). France's third labour confederation, with an 18% share of labour tribunal votes in 1979 and 1982, *FO (Force Ouvrière)*, was founded in 1948 as a breakaway from the militant CGT. Based in the civil service and financial sectors and led since 1963 by André Bergeron, it has traditionally adopted a moderate and conciliatory approach during pay negotiations. The three other significant labour confederations, each enjoying less than 10% of the labour tribunal votes in 1979 and 1982, have been the 250 000-member *CFTC (Confédération Française des Travailleurs Chrétiens)*, a Catholic-based, blue-collar breakaway from the secular CFDT formed in 1964 and led presently by Jean Bornard; the 300 000-member *CGC (Confédération Générale des Cadres)*, a white-collar body orientated towards technicians and lower and middle managers which was founded in 1944 and is led by Paul Marchelli; and the 200 000-member *CSL (Confédération des Syndicats Libres)*, a right-wing 'managers' union' based in the private sector which was originally formed as the *CFT (Confédération Française du Travail)* in 1959 and is led by Auguste Blanc.

The existence of five substantial labour confederations has potentially been a source of strength in labour disputes and in negotiations with the government. However, the low overall unionasation rate in France — which stood at 25% of the total workforce in 1975 (and a substantially lower figure in the private sector) compared to a level of almost 40% in Germany, Italy and Holland, 50% in Britain and more than 80% in Sweden — left union organisations short of funds for administration and welfare and for strikes. Unions are thus very much decentralised in structure, the CGT and CFDT possessing headquarter staffs of barely a hundred, and have been forced to call short, symbolic, 'lightning strikes' and 'days of action' and to resort to violent and obstructive activities rather than to wage protracted, orderly and determined industrial disputes. It has been noticeable that in sectors where incorporation rates have been higher, as in teaching, where the 500 000-member *FEN (Fédération de l'Éducation Nationale)* accounts for 75% of the profession and the *SNI (Syndicat National des Instituteurs)* 90% of primary school teachers, and in agriculture, where the 600 000-member *FNSEA (Fédération Nationale des Syndicats d'Exploitants Agricoles)* represents 50% of farmers[1], labour organisations, with their greater political and economic 'muscle', have been able significantly to influence government policy formation and to improve their conditions and terms of employment. The right-wing FNSEA indeed has been said to 'colonise' the French agricultural ministry during conservative administrations, forcing the grant of special price support subsidies. This has been displayed most graphically recently with the appointment of its leader François Guillaume,

---

[1] Smaller, leftist-leaning, farmers are represented in the 200 000-member, pro-Communist *MODEF (Mouvement pour la Co-ordination et la Défense de l'Exploitation Familiale)* which, based largely in the south, was established in 1959; the *CNSTP (Confédération Nationale des Syndicats de Paysans-Travailleurs)*, which was formed in 1981 and is based primarily in the west; and the pro-Socialist *MONATAR (Mouvement National des Travailleurs Agricoles et Ruraux)*, which was founded in 1975.

a Lorraine dairy farmer, to the post of Agriculture Minister in the Chirac government of March 1986.

During the last decade French trade unions have seen their political influence briefly increase between 1978 and 1983, as government consultation with labour leaders became more frequent and as new legislation was passed which significantly extended union rights. The ability of unions to improve wage and labour conditions for their members diminished, however, as the rapid rise in unemployment ate into union membership rolls and made industrial action increasingly ineffective.

The first impetus to increased consultation between government ministers and trade unions came during the Giscard administration as part of both the President's sincere attempt to broaden participation within the political process and as part of his efforts to gain strict adherence to the belt-tightening process of the 'Barre Plan'. Such efforts, as the CGT's militant activities at Longwy in Lorraine in March 1979 demonstrated, largely failed, however, as a result of both union opposition to the conservative administration's economic programme and to the traditional wariness on the part of French labour leaders of developing too close a relationship with the incumbent government. The election to power of the Socialist Mitterrand administration in 1981 gave significantly greater impetus to the consultation process as, under Jean-Pierre Chevènement, renewed emphasis was given to corporatist economic planning, while a number of trade unionists, including FEN secretary-general André Henry (minister for leisure), were inducted either into the official ministerial team or into ministerial *cabinets*.

The first year of the Socialist administration saw the union movement achieve significant progress towards a number of its long-standing political goals. The statutory minimum wage, *SMIC (Salaire minimum interprofessionel de croissance)*, was substantially increased, the working week was reduced from 40 to 39 hours, with plans being made to reach the long-cherished figure of 35 hours by 1985, and the Auroux act was passed, giving greater protection to union officials and forcing larger firms to involve union leaders in discussions on pay and working conditions. 1981/2 proved in retrospect, however, to be a false dawn for the union movement. During the following three years the Mitterrand administration, abandoning its optimistic expansionary experiment and being forced to call on the aid of the *CNPF (Conseil National du Patronat Français)* employers' federation[1] to reinvest in the private sector, adopted a more conservative economic and social approach and failed to introduce any further significant labour reforms. The CFDT leader Edmond Maire's vision of autogestion, which had been seriously considered by Labour Minister

---

[1] The rightist CNPF, led since 1981 by Yvon Gattaz, officially represents 900 000 firms, but is dominated by larger enterprises. The affiliated *GGPME (Confédération Générale des Petites et Moyennes Enterprises)*, led since 1978 by René Bernasconi, represents small firms.

Jean Auroux in 1982, was quietly shelved, while the CGT's goal of a 35-hour week failed to be realised as a result of disputes over how to fund the transition. Instead, between 1983-86, labour leaders were forced to support the Mitterrand administration in its efforts to fight inflation and restructure and modernise traditional industries, accepting, following the pay explosion of 1982, inflation-indexed wage increases (see Appendix A Table 1) and substantial job-shedding rationalisation as a means of displaying their responsible *solidarité nationale*.

The leaders of the trade unions most closely linked with the incumbent PS-PCF administration, the CGT and CFDT, proved to be most respectful of government demands during 1983. This created a backlash among rank-and-file members and a shift in support within the union movement away from the CGT and CFDT towards the FO and CFTC and particularly towards the white-collar CGC, which militantly opposed the Mitterrand administration's wage restraint policy during 1982/3. This shift was graphically displayed in the results of the elections to the labour tribunal boards in October 1983. The CGT's share of the total vote fell from 37% in 1982 to 28% in 1983 and the CFDT's from 23% to 18%. In contrast, the FO increased its share of the vote from 18% to 25%, the CFTC from 8% to 13% and the CGC from 10% to 16%. Shaken by this decline in support, both the CFDT and CGT responded by adopting a more militant stance during the spring of 1984, the CFDT leading a violent strike at the Talbot car factory at Poissy near Paris in January 1984. The CGT became even more assertive following the termination of the PS-PCF government agreement in July 1984. However, with unemployment mounting, workers became fearful of endangering their jobs through industrial action. The response to the CGT's strike calls proved to be disappointing, with the number of days lost through strike action remaining at an unusually low level during 1984/5.

Between 1982-86 union leaders were forced to adjust to a new, more diminished, political role and to cope with a precipitous decline in their membership rolls, which followed the already substantial contraction experienced between 1978-81. The reduction in union membership resulted not just from the closure and 'rationalisation' of the traditional 'smokestack' and automobile industries, but also as a consequence of the shift in employment towards the less strongly unionised small-firm and service sector. Decline was most marked for the heavy industry-based CGT, whose dues-paying membership was halved to one million between 1979 and 1986. For the CFDT, losses of more than 30% (to 650 000) were recorded during the same period, while membership of the FO, despite energetic recruitment campaigns, fell by 25% to 600 000.[1] Taken as a whole, the French unionisation rate had fallen to a mere 15% in 1986, a rate which was less than half the contemporary rate in West Germany (30%) or Britain

[1] These figures refer to estimates made of actual members and are lower than the 'watered' official figures given out by France's trade unions.

(42%). Only the 'deunionised' United States (15%) among major Western industrialised countries boasted a comparably low level of labour organisation membership.

France's trade union leaders' response to this sudden erosion of their membership was confused and introspective. A number of officials began to reassess their union's role and present activities, proposing the adoption of a more responsive stance towards the introduction of new production technologies and the giving of a greater priority to amenity and welfare services for their organisations' fee-paying members. The most senior union officials, however, grew increasingly dejected and fatalistic. They faced, in addition, after March 1986, a direct and fresh political challenge from the new Chirac administration which sought to introduce a radical new 'efficiency progrmme' aimed at removing many of the administrative restrictions placed upon the free hiring and firing of labour and the use of flexible working hours and to introduce a policy of strict pay restraint for the public sector. The CGT and CFDT formally tabled their opposition to these measures, organising a 'day of protest' in October 1986 directed against the 2-3% wage ceiling. Such responses were, however, largely routine and symbolic, taken without genuine expectation of success. France's main union confederation leaders were thus taken by surprise by the wave of strikes launched spontaneously by rank-and-file members in December 1986 and January 1987, a strike movement which proved to be the most serious industrial challenge to the French state since May 1968. Instead, it was left to small, militant Trotskyist groups, including the *Communist Revolutionary League (LCR)*, *International Communist Party (PCI)* and Arlette Laguiller's *Lutte Ouvrière* (Workers' Struggle), to provide the initial active leadership in both the student protests of November-December 1986 and the railway strike of December 1986 — January 1987. The CGT belatedly, in January 1987, sought to assume control over the striking public sector workers, but was largely unsuccessful. This suggested the growing irrelevance of the older union bodies as effective representatives of French labouring groups.

APPENDIX C

FRENCH OVERSEAS DEPARTMENTS AND TERRITORIES

There are four overseas départements, two overseas *collectivités territoriales* and four overseas territories which form integral parts of the French Republic, returning 22 deputies to the French National Assembly and 13 representatives to the Senate. Each overseas département is administered by its own elected *Conseil général* and *Conseil régional*, each collectivité territoriale by an appointed government commissioner and each overseas territory by an appointed high commissioner who works with locally elected 'territorial assemblies'. The tables below set out salient data concerning these overseas dependencies.

OVERSEAS DÉPARTEMENTS

	Location	(1985) Population	National Assembly Deputies	Senate Represent- atives
FRENCH GUIANA	S America	78 366	2	1
GUADELOUPE	W Indies	328 400	4	2
MARTINIQUE	W Indies	327 073	4	2
RÉUNION	Indian Ocean	530 000	5	2

COLLECTIVITÉS TERRITORIALES

	Location	1985 Population	National Assembly Deputies	Senate Represent- atives
MAYOTTE	Indian Ocean	67 138	1	1
ST PIERRE & MIQUELON	Islands near Newfoundland (N America)	6000	1	1

OVERSEAS TERRITORIES

	Location	1985 Population	National Assembly Deputies	Senate Represent- atives
FRENCH POLYNESIA	S Pacific	164 000	2	1
NEW CALEDONIA	S Pacific	145 000	2	1
SOUTHERN & ANTARCTIC LANDS	Antarctic/ S Indian Ocean	Scientific Base	—	—
WALLIS & FUTUNA ISLANDS	S Pacific	12 391	1	1

In the March 1986 National Assembly election Wallis & Futuna, Mayotte and St Pierre & Miquelon continued to return deputies by the overall majority, two-ballot system in single-member constituencies. Elsewhere the party list, proportional representation electoral system employed in metropolitan France was adopted. In the March 1986 election the RPR (including associates) captured 8 seats, polling strongly in French Polynesia (2 seats) and New Caledonia (2 seats) where the *Front de Libération Nationale Kanake Socialiste (FLNKS)* boycotted the contest; the UDF-CDS won 3 seats (in Mayotte, Martinique and Réunion); 'various right' candidates 1 seat (in Réunion); the PS (including associates) captured 5 seats, including 2 in Martinique and 1 in St Pierre and Miquelon; the PCF 3 seats (2 in Réunion, 1 in Martinique); and 'various left' candidates 1 seat (in Guadeloupe).

Following the decentralisation law of March 1982, Corsica also became a collectivité territoriale with its own directly elected 61-member legislative assembly, which has the power to scrutinise bills passed by the French National Assembly and propose amendments applicable to the island. The island has its own unique, clan-based political system, the dominant parties being: the moderate Radical Party, led by François Giacobbi, which is based in Haute Corse in the north; the Bonapartist Party led by Jean-Paul de Rocca-Serra based in the far south (*Corse du Sud*); the Communist Party led by Dominique Bucchini, which holds the enclave of Sartene in the south; the Socialist Party; the Union for the Corsican People, a moderate autonomist movement; and the Corsican Movement for Autodetermination (MCA), the political wing of the banned Corsican National Liberation Front (FNLC) separatist extremist organisation, which has itself been recently (January 1987) outlawed. Elections to the Corsican legislative assembly in 1982 and 1984 failed to produce a clear party or coalition majority and resulted in the effective paralysis of the regional parliament.

APPENDIX D

THE 1986-1989 SENATE

PARTY STRENGTH IN THE SENATE FOLLOWING THE SEPTEMBER 1986 ELECTIONS

UDF, Centrist, *'divers droite'*	154
RPR (including associates)	77
Socialist Party	64
PCF	15
MRG	9
Total	319[1]

[1] The Senate is gradually being enlarged following approval of a law of 17 June 1983 which decided to increase the number of senators representing French citizens living abroad from six to twelve in 1989 in a step-by-step manner. (Such senators are elected by proportional representation by an electoral college, the *Conseil Supérieur au Français de l'Étranger*). At present ten senators represent French citizens abroad. A further two will be elected in 1989, increasing the size of the Senate to one of 321 members.

APPENDIX E

NATIONAL AND PROVINCIAL NEWSPAPER DISTRIBUTION[1]

NATIONAL DAILY NEWSPAPERS

	c 1983 Circulation
Le Croix (Catholic)	118 000
Le Figaro	331 926
France-Soir	418 830
L'Humanité	150 000
International Herald Tribune	160 709
Libération	135 000
Le Matin de Paris	100 000
Le Monde	360 000
Le Parisien Libéré	351 741

WEEKLY NATIONAL POLITICAL/CURRENT AFFAIRS MAGAZINES

	c 1983 Circulation
Le Canard Enchaîné (Satirical)	500 000
L'Express	585 000
Ici-Paris	700 000
Le Nouvel Observateur	367 101
Paris-Match	912 137
Le Point	328 000

[1] Included are newspapers and political magazines with circulations in excess of 100 000.

132

PRINCIPAL PROVINCIAL DAILY NEWSPAPERS

	Place of Publication	Region	c 1983 Circulation
L'Alsace	Mulhouse	NE	137 035
Centre Presse	Poitiers	Western	123 700
Courrier de l'Ouest	Angers	NW	109 968
Le Dauphine Libéré	Grenoble	SE	382 959
Dépêche du Midi	Toulouse	SW	898 959
Dernières Nouvelles d'Alsace	Strasbourg	NE	240 000
L'Est Républicain	Nancy	NE	255 116
Le Marseillaise	Marseilles	SE	165 000
Le Méridional-la-France	Marseilles	SE	100 000
Midi-Libre	Montpellier	SE	200 000
Le Montagne	Clermont-Ferrand	Central	257 390
Nice-Matin	Nice	SE	263 670
Nord-Éclair	Roubaix	NE	102 773
La Nouvelle République du Centre-Ouest	Tours	Central	273 773
Ouest-France	Rennes	NW	721 404
Paris-Normandie	Rouen	Northern	175 000
Le Progrès	Lyon	Central	353 608
Le Provençal	Marseilles	SE	345 000
Le Républicain Lorrain	Metz	NE	201 936
Sud-Ouest	Bordeaux	SW	365 000
Le Télégramme de Brest et de l'Ouest	Morlaix	NW	203 311
L'Union	Reims	NE	152 000
La Voix du Nord	Lille	NE	371 968

ABBREVIATIONS AND GLOSSARY OF FRENCH TERMS

Action Directe   French anarchist terrorist organisation
arrondissement   district
autogestion   workers' control
'Cabinets'   appointed teams of advisers to individual ministers
CDS   (Centre des Démocrates Sociaux) small centrist party formed in 1976 and part of the UDF; leader Pierre Mehaignerie
CERES   (Centre d'Études, de Recherches et d'Éducation Socialistes) radical faction of Socialist Party (since 1986 known as the 'Socialism and Republic' group); leader Jean-Pierre Chevènement
CFDT   (Confédération Française Démocratique du Travail) pro-Socialist trade union organisation; leader Edmond Maire
CFTC   (Confédération Français des Travailleurs Chrétiens) catholic trade union confederation; leader Jean Bornard
CGC   (Confédération Générale des Cadres) white-collar trade union confederation; leader Paul Marchelli
CGT   (Confédération Générale du Travail) communist trade union confederation; leader Henri Krasucki
changement   political shift from Right to Left or vice versa
Chef du cabinet   head of ministerial 'cabinet'
CIR   (Convention des Institutions Républicaines) 1960s centre-left group led by François Mitterrand
CNIP   (Centre National des Indépendants et des Paysans) centrist grouping; leader Philippe Malaud
CNPF   (Conseil National du Patronat Français) employers' federation; leader Yvon Gattaz
Codefis   (Comités Départementaux pour le Financement) local arms of regional planning
cohabitation   executive power-sharing between Prime Minister and President
Commissaire de la République   successor to state prefect serving in local government
Commissariat au Plan   state 'indicative' planning agency
Conseil d'État   (State Council) judicial review body
Conseil général   elected *département* level general council
Conseiller spécial   presidential special adviser
Conseils restreints   small inter-ministerial meetings
CRS   (Compagnie Républicaine de Sécuritité) state security police
CSL   (Confédération des Syndicats Libres) conservative trade union organisation; leader Auguste Blanc
cumul des mandats   multiple office-holding
DATAR   (Délégation à l'Aménagement du Territoire et à l'Action Régionale) Regional Economic Planning Agency

département   French county
DGSE   (Direction Générale de la Sécurité Extérieure) French intelligence agency
dirigisme   state direction of economic activity
École Normale Supérieure   élite administrative 'grande école' college
École Polytechnique   élite administrative 'grande école' college
Élysée Palace   residence of the French President
EMS   European Monetary System
ENA   (École Nationale d'Administration) national administrative college
énarque   a graduate from the ENA or similar 'grande école'
FEN   (Fédération de l'Éducation Nationale) teachers'/lecturers' education union; leader Jacques Pommatau
FN   (Front National) National Front far-right party formed in 1972; leader Jean-Marie Le Pen
FNSEA   (Fédération Nationale des Syndicats d'Exploitants Agricoles) conservative agricultural union; leader François Guillaume
FO   (Force Ouvrière) autonomous union organisation; leader André Bergeron
force de frappe   French nuclear deterrent
Hôtel Matignon   French Prime Minister's office
IR   (Républicains Indépendants) Independent Republicans, a Giscardian breakaway grouping from the CNIP in 1962
juge d'instruction   examining magistrate
LCR   (Ligue Communiste Révolutionnaire) Communist Revolutionary League, Trotskyist grouping formed in 1974; leader Alain Krivine
majorité   dominant party group or coalition
MRG   (Mouvement des Radicaux de Gauche) centre-left breakaway grouping from the Radical Party; leader Francois Doubin
NIC   Newly Industrialising Country
OAS   (Organisation de l'Armée Secrète) far-right militarist group opposed to Algeria's independence
ORTF   (Office de Radiodiffusion et Télévision Françaises) national broadcasting authority
PCF   (Parti Communiste Français) French Communist Party, formed in 1920; leader Georges Marchais
pieds noirs   French settlers in Algeria
PR   Proportional Representation
PS   (Parti Socialiste) Socialist Party, formed from the SFIO in 1920; leader François Mitterrand, (General-Secretary — Lionel Jospin)
PSU   (Parti Socialiste Unifié) radical-left party grouping formed in 1960; leader Jean-Claude Le Scornet
Quai d'Orsay   French foreign office
questions d'actualité   National Assembly ministerial question time
rigueur   Economic austerity
RP   (Parti Républicain) Republican Party, formed from the IR in 1977; leader François Léotard

RPF (Rassemblement du Peuple Français) Gaullist Party 1947-53
RPR (Rassemblement pour la République) post-1976 neo-Gaullist Party; leader Jacques Chirac, (Secretary-General — Jacques Toubon)
SBA State Broadcasting Authority
SFIO (Section Française de l'Internationale Ouvriere) socialist party formed after split with communists in 1920
tutelle Supervision and control
UDF (Union pour la Démocratie Française) centre-right umbrella organisation formed in 1978; leader Jean Lecanuet
UDR (Union des Démocrates pour la Republique) Gaullist Party 1968-76
UNR (Union pour la Nouvelle Republique) Gaullist Party 1958-67
vote bloqué vote on full text of a parliamentary bill

RECENT BOOKS ON FRENCH POLITICS

M. Adereth   *The French Communist Party*: A Critical History, 1920-1984 (Manchester University Press 1984)

J. Ambler   *The French Socialist Experiment* (Philadelphia: Institute for the Study of Human Issues 1985)

J. Ardagh   *France in the 1980s* (London: Secker & Warburg 1982)

D.S. Bell (Ed)   *Contemporary French Political Parties* (London: Croom Helm 1982)

D.S. Bell and E. Shaw (Eds)   *The Left in France*: Towards the Socialist Republic (Nottingham: Spokesman 1983)

D.S. Bell and B. Criddle   *The French Socialist Party*: Resurgence and Victory (Oxford: Clarendon Press 1984)

D. Cook   *Charles de Gaulle*: A Biography (London: Secker & Warburg 1984)

H.W. Ehrmann   *Politics in France* (Boston: Little, Brown & Co. 1976)

J.E. Flower (Ed)   *France Today* (London: Methuen, 5th edn. 1983)

J.R. Frears   *France in the Giscard Presidency* (London: Allen & Unwin 1981)

J.E.S. Hayward   *Governing France*: The One and Indivisible Republic (London: Weidenfeld & Nicolson, 2nd edn. 1983)

V. Lauber   *The Political Economy of France*: From Pompidou to Mitterrand (New York: Praeger 1983)

H. Machin and V. Wright (Eds)   *Economic Policy and Policy Making under the Mitterrand Presidency, 1981-1984* (London: Frances Pinter 1985)

D. MacShane   *François Mitterrand*: A Political Odyssey (London: Quartet Books 1982)

N. Nugent and D. Lowe (Eds)   *The Left in France* (London: Macmillan 1982)

H.R. Penniman (Ed)   *The French National Assembly Elections of 1978* (Washington D.C.: American Enterprise Institute for Public Policy Research 1980)

D. Pickles   *Problems of Contemporary French Politics* (London: Methuen 1982)

V. Wright   *The Government and Politics of France* (London: Hutchinson, 2nd edn. 1983)

V. Wright (Ed)   *Continuity and Change in France* (London: Allen & Unwin 1984)

CHRONOLOGY OF RECENT EVENTS 1974-1987

1974 April, Pres. Pompidou dies; May, Giscard defeats Mitterrand in presidential election; June, Chirac becomes Prime Minister.

1976 Aug, Chirac resigns as Prime Minister to be replaced by Barre; Sept, 'Barre Plan' introduced; Dec, RPR launched by Chirac.

1977 March, Chirac elected mayor of Paris; May, creation of new Republican Party; Socialist-PCF Union of Left breaks down.

1978 Feb, formation of UDF; March, Right retains its majority in National Assembly elections; April, lifting of price controls.

1979 Jan, Iranian revolution; March, violent disturbances at Longwy (Lorraine); EMS commences operation; June, UDF performs well in European Assembly elections; Dec, USSR invades Afghanistan.

1980 Oct, Iran-Iraq war: oil price hike; Dec, passage of 'Freedom and Security' law and order bill.

1981 Unemployment oversteps 1.5 million; May, Mitterrand defeats Giscard in presidential election; June, Socialists win majority in National Assembly elections: Mauroy Prime Minister, Communists in cabinet; Oct, devaluation and prices/wages freeze; Dec, martial law imposed in Poland.

1982 Jan, decentralisation bill passed; March, nationalisation bill approved; June, devaluation, wages freeze and spending cuts.

1983 March, economic policy U-turn: a major cabinet reshuffle; Aug, French troops sent to Chad.

1984 'Spring of Discontent'; Feb-June, church education demonstrations; June, large losses by the Left in Euro-election: emergence of National Front; July, Fabius replaces Mauroy as Prime Minister in major reshuffle: Communists leave cabinet; Nov, unemployment reaches 2.5 million.

1985 Jan, PCF adopts traditionalist line at 25th Congress; March, large Left losses in local elections; April, change to PR for future Assembly elections: Rocard resigns from cabinet; July, 'Rainbow Warrior' mined in Auckland harbour; Sept, Hernu resigns as Defence Minister; Oct, Socialist Party adopts 'social democratic' line at Toulouse Congress.

1986 March, Right Coalition wins majority in Assembly elections, PS remains the largest single party: Chirac appointed 'cohabitation' Prime Minister; April, easing of price controls; May, PR abolition bill introduced; July, denationalisation bill passed; Sept, Paris terrorism wave; Nov-Dec student demonstrations against 'Loi Devaquet' force climbdown by Chirac; Dec, SNCF rail strike commences.

1987 Jan, public sector strike campaign against wage control; Feb, Giscard announces non-candidature in 1988 presidential election; teachers strike.

Chambers _____ _____ Series

CHAMBERS
WORLD
GAZETTEER

Editor Dr. David Munro

The international directory of facts,
figures, people and places. Over 800 pages
packed with information; 20,000 towns and
cities featured; profiles of every nation in
the world; 150 maps of key political and
administrative divisions; a 120 page atlas in
full colour.

Chambers Commerce Series

The Business of Government

J. Denis Derbyshire

A clear, easy-to-follow explanation of what British government is, how it works in practice and how it influences business procedures.

The Business of Government covers the essential elements of key syllabuses in politics and public administration including BTEC, GCSE, RSA, O/Standard Grade Modern Studies and SCOTVEC plus other modular courses.

- **SIMPLE, READILY UNDERSTOOD LAYOUT**

- **HELPFUL JARGON-FREE LANGUAGE**

- **FREQUENT SELF-ASSESSMENT QUESTIONS**